COGNITIVE REHABILITATION OF CLOSED HEAD INJURED PATIENTS

Cognitive Rehabilitation of Closed Head Injured Patients: A Dynamic Approach

Brenda B. Adamovich, PhD
Director, Speech-Language Pathology Department
John C. Lincoln Hospital and Health Center
Phoenix, Arizona

Jennifer A. Henderson, MS
Assistant Director, Center for Communicative Disorders
Braintree Hospital
Braintree, Massachusetts

Sanford Auerbach, MD
Assistant Professor of Neurology and Psychiatry
Boston University School of Medicine
Boston, Massachusetts

COLLEGE-HILL PRESS, San Diego, California

College-Hill Press
4284 41st Street
San Diego, California 92105

Library of Congress Cataloging in Publication Data

Adamovich, Brenda B.
   Cognitive rehabilitation of closed head injured patients.

   Bibliography: p.
   Includes index.
   1. Cognitive disorders–Patients–Rehabilitation. 2. Brain–Wounds and injuries–Complications and sequelae. 3. Brain damage–Patients–Rehabilitation.
I. Henderson, Jennifer A. II. Auerbach, Sanford. III. Title. IV. Title: Closed head injured patients. [DNLM: 1. Brain Injuries. 2. Brain Injuries–rehabilitation. 3. Cognition Disorders–diagnosis. 4. Cognition Disorders–rehabilitation. WL 354 A199c]
RC553.C64A33   1984   616.8   84-23018
ISBN 0-933014-67-8

Printed in the United States of America

TO Our families, especially Ed, Jack, Marilyn, Bruce, Georgianna, Glenn, and Lynn for their patience, support, and encouragement.

TO Our patients, who aroused our curiosity and inspired this work.

TO Annie Eugenio, for the seemingly endless hours spent typing this manuscript.

PREFACE

The primary purpose of this book is to provide rehabilitation clinicians with unique, well-organized, step-by-step diagnostic and treatment protocols and procedures for head injured patients with diffuse brain lesions. The wide range of deficits encountered in this population was considered. Methods for assessing low through high level cognitive capabilities are described. Emphasis is placed on individual and group therapy tasks and materials.

We have attempted to support techniques designed to facilitate the evaluation and rehabilitation of cognitive skills by sound theoretical foundations and current research. Specifically, we attempted to integrate what is known about neuroanatomical and neurophysiological correlates of cognitive behaviors, such as attention and memory; information processing interrelations with the various stages of problem solving and recall; and normal cognitive development pertinent to breakdowns in mental processing secondary to diffuse brain damage.

TABLE OF CONTENTS

Chapter 1

Introduction

INCIDENCE

Closed head injury has recently been labeled the great "silent epidemic" of our time. It is difficult to assess the true burden that closed head injuries place on our society. Some figures, however, are readily available. The incidence of traumatic head injury in the United States is estimated to be about 200 per 100,000 population per year, which is equivalent to approximately 400,000 such injuries each year. Head injury is the major cause of death in persons under the age of 35 years in the United States (Annegers and Kurland, 1979; Kalsbeek, McLaurin, Harris, and Miller, 1980). The economic cost can be calculated and has been estimated to be about $4 billion per year (Anderson and McLaurin, 1980). The emergence of this "silent epidemic" can be attributed in part to our modern fast-paced lifestyle, which exposes us to the threat of head injury primarily from motor vehicle accidents, and in part to advances in modern medical technology, which increase the chances of survival. The magnitude of this problem is even greater when we realize that a large percentage of survivors are adolescents and young adults with relatively normal life expectancies (Fields, 1976; Kraus, 1980). The problems that emerge from traumatic head injuries persist long after the acute management.

Several terms are used in the literature to describe traumatic brain injuries. Closed head injury is the conventional term for nonpenetrating traumatic injuries of the head that result in cerebral dysfunction. Traumatic brain injury has been advocated by some to place the appropriate emphasis on the brain damage that occurs at the time of injury (Alexander, 1982). Unfortunately, this term does not adequately distinguish between the penetrating injuries that result from missile wounds from the nonpenetrating injuries that usually occur in motor vehicle accidents. For the purpose of this discussion, the term closed head injury will be used to refer to traumatic brain injury occurring as a consequence of nonpenetrating head injuries.

The purpose of this presentation is to describe a conceptual framework that will allow clinicians to interpret the evolving clinical pattern seen in the closed head injury population and to apply appropriate therapeutic techniques for specific behavioral sequelae. The sequelae of closed head injury can be far-reaching. Brain injury can result in physical, psychological, cognitive, and behavioral handicaps. Most workers in the field agree that cognitive and behavioral sequelae make the head injured population particularly difficult to manage and are ultimately the most long-lasting and incapacitating with respect to reintegration into society.

PROBLEMS WITH EXISTING RESEARCH

Unfortunately, two problems emerge as the clinician attempts to structure rehabilitation programs that focus on the neurobehavioral sequelae of closed head injuries. The first, and most obvious, was summarized in a National Institutes of Health (NIH) research status report on the behavioral consequences of closed head injuries, in which Benton (1979) noted that there has been "a paucity of research on the rehabilitation and treatment of closed head patients." Levin, Benton, and Grossman (1982) considered several of these factors in a review of cognitive rehabilitation. They referred to the widely held belief that memory impairment was probably one of the major impediments to rehabilitation in the population and, following a review of the literature on memory retraining, concluded that "a systematic investigation of the effects of memory retraining is a recent development that has yielded mixed feelings with no compelling evidence of general effectiveness" (Levin, Benton, and Grossman, 1982).

Several factors contribute to confound most of the available literature on cognitive rehabilitation: (1) a failure to account for the heterogeneity of the head injured population in terms of lesion distribution, lesion severity, and premorbid abilities; (2) a failure to account for the long course of spontaneous recovery in this population; and (3) the difficulty in randomly allocating a control population to a nontreatment group. The group data approach, particularly with closed head injured persons, does not translate easily into a conceptual framework suitable for the development of rehabilitation programs for specific individuals (Benson and Blumer, 1982).

The "paucity of research" referred to by Benton should be accepted as a challenge to clinicians. All programs that are developed must be grounded in a sound framework that takes into consideration what is known about the neurology and the neuropsychology of traumatic brain injury. More specifically, strategies must be developed that will consider the complex picture of each individual patient.

EARLY INTERVENTION

The value of initiating restorative programs promptly after head injury was demonstrated by a four year project at the Santa Clara Valley Medical Center. As a result of the study, Cope and Hall (1982) reported an estimated savings of $40,000 in hospital costs per patient with early intervention, resulting in earlier attainment of functional goals and leading to more rapid discharge from the hospital. Two groups of severely head injured patients in an acute rehabilitation setting were studied. The early group consisted of 16 patients who were begun on rehabilitation treatment within 35 days following injury. The late group consisted of 20 patients who began rehabilitation treatment more than 35 days following injury. The groups were matched with regard to factors that might bias results, such as age and less morbidity in the early admission groups, including length of coma, level of disability, and neurosurgical procedures required. The results of this study indicated that patients admitted later to rehabilitation programs required twice as much acute rehabilitation as early admission patients and experienced prolonged total rehabilitation periods even though both groups were comparable in initial disability and at outcome would be expected to differ as well. Specific factors considered to be the cause of reduced lengths of stays when rehabilitation is initiated early post injury include the following:

1. Ultimate potential recovery is maximized. Animal studies suggest that "plasticity" and recovery after truma can be related to a specific interval of time after injury. It is suggested that "a missed opportunity to retrain injured neurological mechanisms in a timely fashion may be an opportunity lost forever or available only with greatly increased effort."

2. Medical complications that tend to develop with prolonged residence on most acute medical-surgical wards can be avoided such as decubiti, joint deformities, contractures, and infections.

3. Situations that interfere with recovery of mental functions can be avoided—for example, auditory or visual stimulation can be controlled, the patient's environment and schedule can be organized and maintained, and behaviors and cognitive defects can be dealt with in a consistent manner.

4. Family education and involvement in the rehabilitation process can be initiated.

In summary, the purpose of early rehabilitation programs should be to increase mobility, provide proper stimulation, decrease environmental distractions and provide family education. (Cope and Hall, 1982; Rusk, Block, and Lowman, 1969).

INTERDISCIPLINARY TEAM APPROACH

Rehabilitation of closed head trauma patients is best accomplished when the interdisciplinary team approach is used to provide for the wide variety of behaviors and disabilities exhibited by this population. When possible, team members should routinely include representatives from physiatry, neurology, speech-language pathology, psychology, physical therapy, occupational therapy, nursing, social service, vocational rehabilitation, therapeutic recreation, medical and other consultants as indicated, and family members or significant persons in the patient's life. Cooperation and involvement of family members plays an important role in the rehabilitation process and can determine success or failure of the overall program. Early on, family members must provide background information essential to the establishment of appropriate goals and treatment techniques–for example; interests, likes and dislikes, learning style, previous levels of functioning, premorbid personality, occupation, and level of education. Throughout the rehabilitation process, these individuals must reinforce limitations and capabilities and often the carry over of actual treatment techniques. Successful discharge of a closed head trauma patient often depends on the family's ability to accept and plan for cognitive and behavioral limitations.

Family members have provided a great deal of support for rehabilitation programs locally and nationally. The National Head Injury Foundation, Inc. (18 A Vermont Street, Framingham, Massachusetts 01701), was founded in 1982 by Marilyn Price Spivack, mother of a head injured patient. Over the past few years, this organization has obtained funding for research and services; provided support groups via 20 chapters across the country; become recognized as a consumer voice for head injured persons by many federal agencies and committees; sponsored conferences, become a national clearing house for resources on head injury rehabilitation; and developed a national directory of services. The accomplishments of the National Head Injury Foundation regarding increased public awareness of the problems and needs of closed head injured persons cannot be overemphasized. Clinicians should encourage the establishment of new chapters and should support existing chapters to provide for the needs of the families of their patients.

Chapter 2

Prognostic Considerations

Traditional prognostic approaches in behavioral neurology and rehabilitation have focused on the changes seen in patients with discrete focal lesions. There is a considerable amount of literature on recovery from aphasia associated with discrete focal lesions. However, this information is usually not appropriate with traumatic brain injured patients with multiple, diffuse brain lesions. Although more research is necessary in this area to study specific functions, recovery following closed head trauma generally extends over a longer period of time compared with the recovery period with discrete focal lesions. The prolonged recovery course commonly encountered in cases of severe closed head injury can extend over several years. Reports in the literature refer to recovery periods of six months to decades following injury, with average hospitalized rehabilitation periods of three to six months (Astrom, Eecken, and Adams, 1980; Mackay, 1982; Piller and Gordon, 1981). LeMay and Geschwind (1978) obtained the following results: maximum recovery in children under five years of age following closed head trauma might take decades; people age 20 to 40 years old continued to improve for five to six years following head trauma; middle-aged people, ages 40 to 60 years, improved for two years following injury; and elderly people, beyond age 60 years, generally achieved maximum potential in nine months following injury. Studies of rate of recovery have shown similar variability. It has been suggested that the greatest degree of recovery occurs in the first month, the first two months, or the first six months, with slow progress occurring beyond these periods (Groher, 1977; Gruzzman, 1982). Adamovich and Henderson (1982) reported that the most significant recovery occurred during the first month after initiation of treatment in eight closed head injured subjects whose injuries dated from two to twelve weeks and who received two to four months of cognitive rehabilitation.

Investigators studying recovery following closed head trauma have not consistently controlled for groups of patients with different pathologic conditions and different behavior syndromes, ages, types of treatment, and tests used to measure progress. This failure accounts for some of the variability encountered in studies of outcome and the difficulties in translating the results of long-term follow-up studies into the clinical analysis of individual patients.

COGNITIVE VARIABLES

Conkey (1938) stated that different cognitive functions recovered at differing rates. The recovery of actual function following traumatic brain injury appears to vary with the nature of the function, task complexity, and severity of injury, producing an overall picture of wide variability with some consistent trends in the post traumatic course of these patients (Lezak, 1979). Groher (1977) reported that most improvement on expressive and receptive language skills and on memory tasks occurred during the first month after the patients regained consciousness following closed head injury. However, gradual improvement continued for up to four months, at which time the patients in this investigation were considered to be within normal limits.

Adamovich and Henderson (1983) examined the cognitive abilities of seven head trauma victims at least six months following injury, seven head trauma victims prior to six months following injury, and nine normal control subjects using a battery of 39 diagnostic subtests. Both head injured groups obtained significantly lower scores on tests of recall, yet both groups demonstrated the use of a category recall strategy—that is, they recalled farm animals then jungle animals, and so forth. Both head injured groups had significantly more difficulty than the normal control group in giving antonyms. The two groups differed with regard to the type of error response made. The group six months following trauma gave no response or related responses; for example, they supplied "brother" in response to "daughter." The group prior to six months following trauma, on the other hand, added the words "not to"—that is, they answered "not to lend" in response to "lend."

The prior to six months following trauma group performed significantly more poorly than did the normal group on: (1) the reading tests administered and on tests of verbal and graphic naming; error responses revealed no consistent patterns across subjects; (2) describing verbal absurdities due to an inability to identify the most salient features or a tendency to consider the problem in concrete inappropriate ways; (3) describing differences of items—for example, "How are physicians and surgeons different?" The subjects were able to correctly describe likenesses of items. This group performed significantly more poorly than the six months following injury group on memory tests, visual and verbal sequencing tasks, problem solving, and task-specific insight.

Hagen and Malkmus (1979) described levels of cognitive functioning that form a hierarchy of behavioral stages through which a head injured person can progress as recovery occurs. The scale is used to identify a patient's highest level of cognitive functioning continuously throughout the rehabilitation period. The cognitive levels and expected behaviors are presented in Table 2-1.

PHYSICAL VARIABLES

The best-known prognostic studies have been those of Jennett and Bond (1975), in which Bayes' theorem was applied sequentially in such a way that prognostic factors were assumed to be statistically independent. Jennett and Bond reported that this assumption was not valid with head injured patients. Instead, a logical regression model was proposed to permit comparative assessments of the relative power of input variables and the interactions between the variables that determine the prognosis. Specific prognostic indicators include length of coma; duration of posttraumatic amnesia; age; location, extent and severity of cerebral damage; presence of seizures; and medical complications.

Coma

The duration of coma is considered by many to be the best prognostic indicator of functional recovery. During deep coma, psychological and motor responses to stimulation are completely lost. In moderately deep coma, psychological and motor responses are reduced to only rudimentary or reflex motor responses with an absence of any psychological, understandable responses to external stimulation or internal need. During coma, intellectual contact with the patient cannot be made. The patient does not respond verbally or motorically to simple verbal commands (Warren, Hubbard, and Knox, 1977; Whitaker and Ojemann, 1977). The Glasgow Coma Scale, designed by Jennett and his associates (Jennett and Bond, 1975; Jennett, Snoak, Bond, and Brooks, 1981) predicts recovery after closed head trauma by rating the degree of eye opening, the best verbal response, and the best motor response. This scale is presented in Table 2-2.

The Glasgow Outcome Scale has five categories (0 to 4), ranging from good recovery to a persistent vegetative state (Jennett et al, 1981).

Whitaker and Ojemann (1977) suggested the following ratings of coma: (1) the patient is awake and responsive to commands on admission with momentary loss of consciousness occurring at the time of impact and with no resulting neurological deficits, (2) coma does not exceed 24 hours, or (3) coma exceeds 24 hours. It has also

**Table 2-1. Rancho Los Amigos Scale of Cognitive Levels
and Expected Behavior**

Level I	No Response	Unresponsive to all stimuli
Level II	Generalized Response	Inconsistent, nonpurposeful, non-specific reactions to stimuli. Responds to pain, but response may be delayed.
Level III	Localized Response	Inconsistent reaction directly related to type of stimulus presented. Responds to some commands. May respond to discomfort.
Level IV	Confused, Agitated Response	Disoriented and unaware of present events with frequent bizarre and inappropriate behavior. Attention span is short and ability to process information is impaired.
Level V	Confused Inappropriate Nonagitated Response	Nonpurposeful random or fragmented responses when task complexity exceeds abilities. Patient appears alert and responds to simple commands. Performs previously learned tasks but is unable to learn new ones.
Level VI	Confused, Appropriate Response	Behavior is goal-directed. Responses are appropriate to the situation with incorrect responses due to memory difficulties.
Level VII	Automatic, Appropriate Response	Correct routine responses which are robotlike. Appears oriented to setting, but insight, judgment and problem-solving are poor.
Level VIII	Purposeful, Appropriate Response	Correct responding, carryover of new learning. No required supervision, poor tolerance for stress, and some abstract reasoning difficulties.

From Hagen, C., and Malkmus, D. Intervention strategies for language disorders secondary to head trauma. American Speech-Language-Hearing Association, Short courses, Atlanta, 1979.

Table 2-2. Glasgow Coma Scale

Eyes	Open	Spontaneously	4
		To verbal command	3
		To pain	2
	No response		1
Best motor Response	To verbal command	Obeys	6
	To painful stimulus	Localizes pain	5
		Flexion – withdrawal	4
		Flexion – abnormal (decerebrate rigidity)	3
		Extension (decerebrate rigidity)	2
		No response	1
Best verbal response		Oriented and converses	5
		Disoriented and converses	4
		Inappropriate words	3
		Incomprehensible sounds	2
		No response	1
TOTAL			3-15

From Jennett, B., Snoak, J., Bond, M., and Brooks, N. Disability after severe head injury: Observations on the use of the Glasgow Outcome Scale. *Journal of Neurology, Neurosurgery, and Psychiatry*, 44:285-293, 1981. Reprinted with permission.

been reported that severe brain injury results if coma lasts more than six hours. Head injured patients who were in coma beyond seven days often do not recover to preinjury status even if they are younger than 20 years of age. Lezak (1979) studied two groups of patients: (1) those who were unconscious for less than two weeks and; (2) those who were unconscious for two weeks or more. On every measure, the more severely injured subjects performed more poorly. However, this severely injured group displayed a considerable but nonsignificant improvement initially following coma.

Brooks, Aughton, Bond, and their associates (1980) suggested that patients who were in coma for three months or less had a good prognosis for recovery. In this study, the majority of patients under 20 years of age were ambulatory with or without equipment and most were independent. If they had been in coma more than 13 weeks, the prognosis was poorer but variable. Finally, if they had been in coma over four months, independent living occurred only in unusual cases.

Posttraumatic Amnesia

Posttraumatic amnesia is defined as the period following brain injury during which the patient does not have continuous memory for ongoing events in daily life. Patients have difficulty with orientation and learning. The greater the diffuse damage, the longer the duration of posttraumatic amnesia. The Galveston Orientation and Amnesia Test (GOAT) evaluates the major spheres of orientation (time, place, person); interval of posttraumatic amnesia; and retroactive amnesia or the interval preceding the injury for which no events are recalled. Levin, O'Donnell, and Grossman (1979) reported that the duration of posttraumatic amnesia, as determined by the Galveston Orientation and Amnesia Test, was longer in patients with diffuse or bilateral brain injuries than in patients with focal, unilateral brain lesions. Eight per cent of the patients with posttraumatic amnesia lasting less than four weeks had ipsilateral paresis. More than half of the patients studied (104 patients of 175 patients) with posttraumatic amnesia had suffered impact on the right side of the brain.

Mandleberg (1976) suggested that the cognitive level of functioning is more generally related to the severity of head injury only in relatively early stages of recovery. The critical period at which the posttraumatic amnesia may cease to be a useful predictor of cognitive levels was suggested to be three to six months for verbal skills and seven to twelve months for nonverbal skills. It was also suggested that the duration of posttraumatic amnesia had no implication for eventual outcome of cognitive levels. Long periods of posttraumatic amnesia correlated significantly with impaired memory function but not with changes in personality or with the development of symptoms of mental illness following trauma. The duration of posttraumatic amnesia was closely associated with degree of social, mental, and neurophysical disability. Deficits occurred in all areas following posttraumatic amnesia and when the amnesia lasted longer than 24 hours, severe brain injury, resulted; when amnesia lasted longer than seven days there was very severe brain injury. Bever (1975) suggested the following scale of posttraumatic amnesia: (1) Less than five minutes – very mild deficits; (2) less than one hour – mild deficits; (3) 1 to 24 hours – moderate deficits; (4) one to seven days – severe deficits; (5) longer than seven days – very severe deficits; and (6) longer than four weeks, extremely severe deficits.

Age

Wetzel and Squire (1982) suggested that age strongly influences physical and mental sequelae of head injury. Heiskanen and Sipponen (1970) reported that mortality and social morbidity increased significantly in patients over 60 years old compared with those patients under 20 years old following head injury. Levin (1981) found that older patients did significantly more poorly than younger patients on more difficult memory tasks of the Wechsler Adult Intelligence Test. On the other hand, Lezak (1979) studied two age groups: patients under 25 years old and patients over 25. No difference was found on tests administered to these two groups of head injured patients.

Medical Complications

Brooks and colleagues (1980) found a poor prognosis, particularly with reference to motor activity, for patients experiencing intracranial mass lesions (epidural, subdural, and intracerebral hematomas and focal swelling of brain) that required surgical decompression and modification of the mass. Skull fractures reportedly have little significance in establishing a prognosis. Generally, the more extensive the brain damage the poorer the prognosis. The extent of verbal and motor function damage on hospital admission is thought to be directly related to the probability of subsequent neuropsychological deficits, which, in turn, are directly related to the severity of injury (Whitaker and Ojemann 1977).

Medical complications that can result in a poor prognosis for returned function are anoxia, intracranial pressure, electrolyte imbalance, cerebral edema, intracranial hemorrhages, increased or decreased blood pressure, hyperthermia, and the presence of seizures (Gazzaniga and Hillyard, 1971; Mackay, 1982; Whitaker and Ojemann, 1977).

BEHAVIORAL AND PSYCHOLOGICAL VARIABLES

Premorbid personality and behaviors impact on recovery. Individuals who were strong-willed, self-motivated, and driven to accomplish positive goals with good track records (school and work history) tend to do better. Premorbid factors that are poor prognostic indicators include emotional and psychological instability, history of alcohol or drug abuse, poor work and school history, and general lack of motivation to accomplish productive goals.

Greater recovery occurs when families or significant others are supportive and involved in the rehabilitation process with regard to reinforcing treatment programs, recognizing limitations in dealing with the patient's denial of deficits, creating home and community environments conducive to recovery of functions that continually change as recovery occurs, and providing continual encouragement, concern, and love even in the most difficult periods.

RETURN TO WORK

Work capacity and impairment of leisure pursuits were the aspects of daily life chiefly affected by closed head injury. Wetzel and Squire (1982) found that 60.5 per cent of the patients studied were actively functioning back at work according to their abilities. Fifty-four patients in the age range of 16 to 39 years were studied. Only 22 of 45 patients who were working before the injury returned to work full time four to six months following the accident. The trend for those returning to work was a lesser degree of satisfaction with the job following the accident. The eight patients who did not return to work all had physical disabilities. They tended to be more severely impaired and also showed a decrease in social activity. In general, factors that are poor prognostic indicators regarding the patient's ability to return to work following closed head trauma include increased age; longer posttraumatic amnesia; previous personality deficits, such as alcoholism or emotional instability; gross physical handicaps, nonsupportive families or significant others; low premorbid intelligence; no professional training or higher education premorbidly; longer periods of coma; nonsupportive employers; and premorbid jobs that required speed, safety, and efficiency (Heiskanen and Sipponen, 1970; Rusk, Block, and Lowman, 1969). It is difficult to motivate a patient to return to work if his or her disability benefits from previous employment are greater than the patient would receive by accepting a lower paying job that was more in line with his or her cognitive abilities. Head injured individuals also receive little work gratification if they are capable of doing only simpler, nondemanding jobs following their accidents. The denial of disability experienced by most head injured patients also interferes with their willingness to accept lower level positions.

Heiskanen and Sipponen (1970) studied the effect of coma and length of coma and age on the patient's ability to return to work. Of patients unconscious for 24 hours, 70 per cent of patients younger than 20 years of age returned to work, whereas only 30 per cent of the patients older than age 50 years returned to work. No patients who were unconscious for more than a month returned to work. Of those patients unconscious for one week, no patients over 40 years of age returned to work.

When a patient reaches a high enough level of cognitive functioning, vocational counseling is a very important step in the rehabilitation process. Occupational training must often include psychotherapy to improve the patient's acceptance of his or her disabilities and to set appropriate vocational goals; training with equipment that might be required for the position, such as calculators, typewriters, and so forth; training on actual work tasks and on-the-job observations by the clinician. The patients who are most successful in returning to work accept jobs that are routine and that require no problem-solving once the job is learned through repetition of the actual tasks requried. Unfortunately, ideal job conditions for severely damaged patients do not exist. Head injured patients must be fit, often inappropriately, into services designed for elderly or mentally retarded individuals even though head injured patients are often capable of being more productive than individuals in these other groups.

Existing programs for closed head trauma patients with a high level of cognitive functioning that are geared to returning to work have stringent entrance requirements, such as high IQ levels, cooperative families, and no emotional or motivational problems. While these are helpful for the patients who meet the entrance requirements, many patients are left without services. Generally, there is a serious lack of facilities and services for head injured patients at all levels.

Chapter 3

Neuroanatomical and Neurobehavioral Considerations

NEUROPATHOLOGY OF CLOSED HEAD INJURY

Recent advances in the study of the neuropathological changes associated with closed head injury provide a unique opportunity to develop a useful neurobehavioral classification system. Several excellent reviews of this literature are available (Brooks and Aughton, 1976; Gruzzman, 1982; Waterhouse and Fein, 1982). The purpose of this chapter is to address the processes underlying neurobehavioral changes.

The pathophysiology of closed head injury is closely related to the pathophysiology of concussion. It is, therefore, worthwhile to briefly define concussion. A special committee was recently formed to study head injury nomenclature. They defined concussion as "a clinical syndrome characterized by immediate and transient impairment of neural function, such as alteration of consciousness, disturbance of vision, equilibrium, etc., due to mechanical force" (Committee to Study Head Injury Nomenclature, 1966).

The study of concussion actually began to emerge in the nineteenth century with the Industrial Revolution and the evolution of the railway (Trimble, 1981). This historical era is noteworthy because it represented the point in time when people became exposed to the high-speed acceleration or deceleration injuries that can accompany railway collisions. As the railway system evolved, engines became more powerful, train speeds increased, travel by railway became more popular, and closed head injuries with concussion became more common. The litigation that accompanied these troublesome injuries evoked medicolegal concerns, which certainly contributed to the general interest in the mysterious pathophysiology of closed head injury and its sequelae. Nineteenth century explanations translating mechanical trauma into alterations in neural function were somethat limited. Many of these limitations were imposed by technical shortcomings and a lack of appropriate experimental material. Early explanations emphasized the role of vibration in causing rupture of small blood vessels or the direct damage of brain tissue (Trimble, 1981). Throughout most of the nineteenth century, concussion was generally thought to be related to the movement or shaking up of brain contents (ébranlement of the French), although some favored vasomotor disturbances as the underlying cause (Courville, 1953).

It was probably the work of Denny-Brown and Russell (1941) that heralded the evolution of current approaches to the pathophysiology of closed head injury. Based on experimental studies, these authors pointed out that an acceleration-deceleration force was instrumental in the induction of an immediate loss of consciousness after a closed head injury. Blunt injury to a stationary head could produce brain damage, but not necessarily an immediate loss of consciousness. Although they were unable to demonstrate clearly the pathologic basis of loss of consciousness, they did stress the role of impaired brain stem reflexes. In the decade that followed, other researchers elaborated on their observations. Groat and Simmons (1950) further suggested that all concussions were associated with cell loss in the brain stem even if the concussions were mild.

The work done in this period helped to draw attention to several key factors necessary to understand closed head injury: (1) closed head injury may be associated with either of two types of trauma — that caused by a blunt force to a stationary head or that caused by an acceleration-deceleration injury; (2) the immediate loss of consciousness found in many cases of closed head injuries is associated with the acceleration-deceleration type of injury; and (3) brain stem pathology likely accounts for the loss of consciousness.

Holburn (1943), a physicist, devised a model to account for the development of widespread pathology from an impact on a single point on the skull. He used a gelatin model in a skull to demonstrate that "shear strains" in the gelatin became more visible on forward rotation. Such shear strains were greatest in the frontotemporal region and were more apparent when the head was forced to move. In addition, Holburn speculated that the immediate loss of consciousness may be attributed to a "diffuse neuronal injury" in a particular brain region. His model was confirmed in experimental animal models by Pudenz and Sheldon (1946) and later refined by the experimental studies of Ommaya and Gennarelli (1974).

Another major contribution was the observation by Strich (1961) of widespread microscopic white matter lesions in the brains of patients with severe head injuries. These lesions were demonstrated in cases in which there were no apparent cortical lesions that could account for the white matter lesions or the profound degree of symptoms. Although Strich's initial observations and interpretations were not widely accepted (Adams and Victor, 1977), they provided the basis for some interpretations of the pathophysiology of minor head injury (Oppenheimer, 1968), in which cortical lesions were not easily documented. More importantly, her observations helped to raise the speculation that the widespread white matter lesions could be considered separately from multiple cortical lesions and other secondary lesions. The latter point has become more apparent with recent experimental data.

Recent clinical and experimental studies have followed along the lines of these earlier works. The forces involved in a closed head injury can be considered to be two types: direct impact or inertial. Direct impact forces usually result in discrete focal lesions. Contusions may be found at the site of direct impact or, as the brain shifts in relation to the skull, contusions may be found at sites remote from the point of direct impact. These remote contusions or contrecoup lesions can be found in the frontotemporal distribution predicted by Holburn's model (1943). The distribution of these contusions relates to the rotational forces and to contact of the brain surface with certain bony prominences in the skull. It might be expected that cortical contusions would occur in a distribution that varied with the exact circumstances of injury. In fact, certain generalizations emerge from clinical and experimental reviews: (1) focal contusions or lacerations occur under the point of impact if there is a severe local deformity, depressed skull fracture; (2) contusions generally occur in a predictable pattern that is independent of the site of impact (frontopolar, orbitofrontal, and anterior temporal lobes, and sylvian fissure); and (3) contusions are commonly bilateral but asymmetrical (Adams, Scott, Parker, Graham and Doyle, 1980); Clifton, Grossman, Makala, et al., 1980; Ommaya and Gennarelli, 1974). It is now generally acknowledged that acceleration-deceleration injuries are responsible for the predominant pathologic lesion in traumatic closed head injuries. More specifically, the head is accelerated and then suddenly stopped. The forces involved may be translational when movement is in a horizontal plane or angular when there is a rotational component, usually about the diencephalic-midbrain junction. It is generally accepted that the angular acceleration injury is most effective in producing the diffuse injury and the concussion associated with closed head injury.

Diffuse axonal injury (widespread damage to axons in the white matter of the brain) occurs secondary to acceleration forces. In neuropathological studies of fatal nonmissile injuries in humans,

Adams, Graham, Murray, and Scott (1982) have demonstrated that diffuse axonal injury is associated with a triad of pathological changes: "focal lesions in the corpus callosum and in the dorsolateral quadrant of the rostral brain stem in the area of the superior cerebellar peduncle, and microscopic evidence of diffuse damage to axons," especially in parasagittal and rostral midbrain areas. It is of some interest to note that the presence and severity of this diffuse axonal injury do not correlate with the presence and severity of cortical contusions. In fact, cortical contusions were more commonly associated with fatal nonmissile head injuries without diffuse axonal injury. Similarly, the markers associated with focal cortical contusions (skull fractures) were more commonly found in the latter group without diffuse axonal injury. It seems that cortical contusions were more commonly encountered in falls and direct blows to the head, whereas diffuse axonal injury was more commonly encountered in high-speed acceleration-deceleration injuries, such as motor vehicle accidents.

Gennarelli and his colleagues (Gennarelli, Adams, and Graham, 1981; Gennarelli, Thibault, Adams, et al., 1982) complemented the work of Adams, Graham, and Gennarelli (1981) with experimental studies and added an additional unifying concept. They subjected groups of subhuman primates to head acceleration without impact. In the earlier experiments, using short acceleration pulses, they produced mild concussions with contusions in the frontal and temporal lobes and occasional intracerebral hemorrhages. Increasing the acceleration succeeded only in increasing the incidence of subdural hematomas. Finally, increasing the duration of the acceleration pulse produced prolonged unconsciousness and severe diffuse axonal injury. Therefore, it was the length of the acceleration pulse that appeared to be critical in the production of diffuse axonal injury and the characteristic triad of focal lesions and microscopic evidence already described. In a recent review of their experimental studies of head injury in animals, Sekino, Nakamura, Satoh, Kikuchu, and Sanada (1981) also came to a conclusion similar to that of Gennarelli and colleagues. They noted that contusional lesions were more closely associated with impacts of short duration, whereas concussional injuries (loss of consciousness without cortical contusion) were associated with impacts of longer duration. Sekino and associates differ, however, in suggesting that the conditions that result in brain contusions are very close to those causing concussions in humans. It may be conjectured that most blows and short falls result primarily in the contusions encountered either with direct impact injury or with short pulse acceleration-deceleration injuries. Motor vehicle accidents, on the other hand, are more analogous to the longer pulse acceleration injuries and are more closely associated with the development of diffuse axonal injury.

Additional observations emerged from the work of Gennarelli and co-workers: (1) the severity of the posttraumatic coma correlates with the severity of the diffuse axonal injury: (2) diffuse axonal injury was associated with a gradient of severity (focal midbrain lesions occurred only when the injury was severe enough to produce focal callosal lesions); (3) small contusions were associated only occasionally with diffuse axonal injury (interestingly, these contusions were restricted to the junction of the CA1 region and the subiculum in the hippocampus); and (4) laterally directed accelerations were more effective in the production of diffuse axonal injury than were accelerations directed in sagittal or oblique directions.

To summarize, it seems that two classes of lesions can be directly associated with closed head injury. Focal cortical contusions are associated with direct impact (a short acceleration pulse, such as may be encountered in falls) and are generally found in the frontal (frontopolar and orbitofrontal) and temporal (anterior temporal, but not necessarily medial temporal) lobes. Diffuse axonal injury of the white matter is associated with high acceleration injuries (long acceleration pulses, such as occur in motor vehicle accidents). The severity of diffuse axonal injury correlates with the severity of the posttraumatic coma and is associated with focal lesions in the corpus callosum and the dorsolateral quadrants of the midbrain.

Certain secondary pathological changes are not uncommonly seen in the closed head injury population. Traumatic head injury may be associated with a tearing of small vessels over the surface of the brain, resulting in either subdural or epidural hematomas. The small microscopic and sometimes hemorrhagic white matter lesions may result in larger intracerebral hemorrhages. The edema or swelling of the brain that may result in response to widespread cerebral trauma may lead to compression and occlusion of larger cerebral blood vessels and to subsequent infarction. Edema may also result in direct compression of brain stem structures with additional life-threatening consequences. Cardiopulmonary compromise may result in secondary cerebral hypoxia. Optimal acute care management necessitates aggressive management of all of the secondary problems. As modern medical technology and care delivery systems have evolved, the secondary group of lesions are less a factor in the neurobehavioral sequelae of head injury.

Most of the secondary pathological lesions contribute to one of three types of syndromes. The focal vascular lesions often produce syndromes that are recognizable because of the abundant literature on the neurobehavioral sequelae of focal lesions. Compression resulting from either edema or a hematoma may produce either a focal ischemic type injury or a brain stem compression injury. If the latter is not treated, death may result. However, the relative contribution of brain stem pathology from a near-herniation is always difficult to compute in individual cases. Finally, the possibility of hypoxia must be considered. In a review of hypoxic ischemic changes in fatal nonmissile head injuries, Graham, Adams, and Doyle (1978) highlighted the frequency of this problem in cases in which there was a clear history of cardiopulmonary compromise.

In conclusion, it must be kept in mind that lesions secondary to contusions and diffuse axonal injury must be considered in the evaluation of individual cases. It seems fair to say, however, that the secondary lesions will be minimal in survivors treated optimally in the acute care setting.

NEUROBEHAVIORAL CONSIDERATIONS

Attention

Disorders of attention can be seen in patients with frontal lobe lesions as well as the widespread diffuse axonal injuries associated with acceleration-deceleration accidents. Clinically, it may not be possible to distinguish these entities. A potential explanation for attentional deficits following diffuse axonal injuries can be obtained from experimental models (Adams, Graham, and Gennarelli, 1981; Gennarelli et al., 1981, 1982). Injuries producing primarily diffuse axonal injuries are associated with immediate and prolonged coma. Anatomically, the elements of the reticular activating system ascend to the frontal lobe systems and the medial forebrain bundle. Two main components of the frontolimbic system may be involved differentially in frontal lobe disorders that emerge due to frontotemporal contusions or diffuse axonal injury. A modern view of the limbic system recognizes the existence of two antagonistic systems (Livingston and Escobar, 1972). The medial limbic system refers to (1) the classic Papez circuit (1937) linking the hypothalamus, anterior thalamic nuclei, cingulate gyrus, and hippocampus; (2) the strong connections to the brain stem reticular activating core described by Nauta (1958); and (3) the cortical component of this system, which generally includes the dorsolateral prefrontal granular cortex. The basolateral component of the limbic system was emphasized by Yakolev (1948) and includes orbitofrontal cortex, insular and anterior temporal areas together with their connections with the amygdala, and the magnocellular portion of the dorsomedial nucleus of the thalamus. The basolateral system receives convergent sensory input from both the parietal lobes and the olfactory pathways (Powell, 1972). Anatomical considerations suggest that the medial limbic circuit is particularly concerned with activity in the reticular core; whereas the basolimbic system is more concerned with the functions of the sensory-receptive and interpretive cortex. Anatomically the medial limbic and basolateral limbic systems are generally distinct. Although there are no direct connections between the two circuits, they do have a convergence of outflow at the septal, hypothalamic, and midbrain levels (Nauta, 1960). Thus it appears that the two circuits may function as mutual antagonists on behavioral outflow pathways (Livingston and Escobar, 1972).

Extensive lesions of the medial limbic systems have been characterized principally by psychic and motor hypoactivity. Clinical syndromes of akinesia, mutism, and apathy have been reported with lesions of these pathways (Neilson, 1953). Stimulation or irritative disorders of the medial limbic system may presumably lead to the opposite behavioral effect. Stimulation of the dopaminergic mesolimbic system in rats results in fearfulness and hiding (Stevens and Livemore, 1978). The suggestion that psychiatric disorders characterized by restlessness, anxiety, irritability, and obsessive-compulsive behavior may reflect hyperactivity of the medial limbic system has contributed to the rationale for producing selective destructive lesions in the cingulate gyrus or medial frontal quadrants in the management of such disorders (Ballantine, Cassidy, Flanagan, et al., 1967; Brown and Lighthill, 1968; Foltz, 1968; LeBeau, 1952).

Lesions in the orbital-frontal-insular-anterior temporal or basolateral system usually result in disinhibition and hyperactivity. Selective lesions in the orbitofrontal portion of this system have been found effective in relieving some cases of intractible depressive syndromes (Knight, 1965). The anterior temporal cortex also receives a considerable amount of convergent sensory information. There is some reason to suspect that it is a disturbance of this limbic component that might be involved in the altered sensory perception and interpretation that might be encountered in a variety of psychiatric disorders (Livingston and Escobar, 1972).

It must be remembered that the prefrontal cortex represents the suprastructure of the limbic system (Nauta, 1962) and may prove to be a key to analyzing the impact of dysfunction in either of these systems. Recent reviews of the neuropsychological literature of frontal lobe syndromes have emphasized the existence of two distinct syndromes: the dorsolateral syndrome and orbitofrontal syndrome (Stuss and Benson, 1983). This literature is relevant to the present discussion because it divides the frontal lobe along the lines of their representations of the mesolimbic (dorsolateral frontal lobe) and basolateral (orbitofrontal) limbic systems.

The changes associated with dorsolateral and orbitofrontal pathology influence personality changes, motor performance, and cognitive abilities in a parallel manner. For instance, the dorsolateral syndrome is characterized by "pseudodepressed" state with a lack of spontaneity, apathy, hypokinesia, slowness, and a lack of initiative (Blumer and Benson, 1975). These changes are especially reflected in motor performance. Memory performance is limited by interference effects and the subject is believed to suffer from a difficulty in sustaining attention to relevant elements (Fuster, 1980). In addition, there may be impaired performance on tests of verbal fluency; some small decrements may occur on formal IQ scores; and verbal regulation of behavior is impaired (Stuss and Benson, 1984). These findings are comparable to findings in animal studies and are compatible with medial limbic system deficits.

Orbitofrontal lesions are generally associated with a disinhibition of stimulus-response interactions (Gazzaniga, 1979). The associated personality disorder is often described as "pseudopsychopathic," with hyperactivity, sexual disinhibition, self-indulgent activity, and inappropriate social behavior. Paranoid and grandiose thinking may also be present (Blumer and Benson, 1975). Motor behavior is generally characterized as restless, impulsive, explosive, and hyperactive (Stuss and Benson, 1984). Interference effects are found on memory testing, but, in the orbitofrontal group, they are attributed to an inability to suppress interfering stimuli (Fuster, 1980). Unlike the dorsolateral syndrome, verbal fluency, IQ testing, and the verbal regulation of behavior are generally unchanged (Stuss and Benson, 1983).

It is now possible to apply this neuropsychological model of frontolimbic disorders to our understanding of the pathophysiology of closed head injuries. The frontotemporal contusions encountered in closed head injuries usually involve orbitofrontal and anterior temporal regions or the basolateral limbic system. These lesions likely account for the "positive" symptoms seen in this population (hyperactivity, distractibility, disinhibition, paranoia). The second class of lesions, seen with long pulse angular acceleration injuries resulting in medial limbic system disorders with midbrain lesions, likely accounts for the immediate coma, posttraumatic confusion, and subsequent "negative" symptoms of apathy, inattention, slowness, and long latency. In this model, it is likely that the basolateral syndrome can be attributed to the cortical contusions· and the medial limbic syndrome to midbrain pathology (the caudal extent of the medial limbic system). According to Auerbach, Moore, and Weinberg (1984), it is also likely that recovery in these areas proceeds at different rates, with the basolateral disorders reaching a plateau within a shorter period of time than the medial limbic disorder.

Organization

Disorders of spatial organization can be nonlocalizing and are found in patients with focal lesions as well as confusional disorders of diverse causations. Hemi-inattention and specific sensory modality inattention are not commonly seen in the closed head injury patient unless there is an additional focal lesion.

Memory

Brierly (1977) suggested that the usual pattern of cortical contusion following closed head injury does not include the medial temporal lobes, which have been implicated by some as the possible site of focal lesions that may produce amnesia. On the other hand, Sekino and associates (1981) reported that focal medial temporal lesions may at times occur as a consequence of a contusional lesion or temporal lobe hematoma or by occlusion of a posterior cerebral artery (as may occur with downward herniation). Different types of memory disturbances have been reported with left versus right temporal lesion. It has been reported that memory deficits for verbal material occur following left hemisphere temporal lobe damage, and memory deficits for visual, spatial, nonverbal material occur following right hemisphere temporal lobe damage, regardless of an auditory of visual input modality. Thus, the type of material being stored, rather than the sensory modality, differentiates the right from the left hemisphere temporal lobes (Goodglass and Kaplan, 1979; Kimura, 1961; Milner, 1967, 1968, 1971).

Gennarelli and colleagues (1982), suggested that minor contusional lesions in the hippocampus may accompany severe diffuse axonal injuries caused by closed head trauma. Gennarelli concluded, however, that contusions observed in the hippocampus were relatively minor. Recent animal studies have demonstrated that minor hippocampal lesions are probably not sufficient to cause a significant impairment in memory (Mahut, Zda-Morgan, and Moss, 1982).

The hippocampal complex is sensitive also to hypoxia. Graham and co-workers (1978) observed ischemic-hypoxic damage in the hippocampal region of brains of patients with fatal nonmissile injuries. It should be remembered that these findings were generally associated with a clear history of cardiopulmonary compromise. It is difficult to exclude the possibility that an ischemic hippocampal lesion contributes to the clinical picture. Hippocampal lesions have been reported to cause the following memory disturbances: (1) failure of memory for recent events with intact remote memory; and (2) good digit span recall with an inability to learn verbal material presented aurally or visually (Goodglass and Kaplan, 1979).

PHARMACOTHERAPY

The adverse side effects of medications can exacerbate a tendency for head trauma patients to become confused. Two areas of special concern in the treatment of the head injured are discussed: agitation and intellectual recovery.

Agitation is not an uncommon problem that may limit therapy, particularly in the early stages of recovery. In general, behavioral management is the optimal method to treat agitation. In some cases, however, agitation becomes a major problem, which limits the ability of the staff to work with the patient. The patient's safety and the safety of other patients must also be considered. When these situations arise, the major tranquilizers can be useful. Caution should be exercised in their use. Patients should be started on a low dose, and the dose should be carefully titrated to the needs of the patient. Furthermore, the clinician must continue to titrate the medication as the patient's condition will continue to evolve and the need for major tranquilizers may cease.

Even when the major tranquilizers are used judiciously, the clinician should be aware of some theoretical problems. Several experimental studies using animal models of brain damage have suggested that the use of major tranquilizers may delay the course of recovery (Feeney, Gonzalez, and Law, 1982). Furthermore, the sedative effects of these agents may contribute to the confusional state that may underlie much of the agitation. On the other hand, poorly managed agitation may delay therapeutic intervention and rehabilitation. Other medications (beta blockers, antihistamines, tricyclics, antidepressants, lithium carbonate, benzediazepenes, and so forth) are unreliable and generally ineffective in the early management of agitation in these patients.

The observation that the major tranquilizers may delay recovery of function has even greater implications to cognitive rehabilitation. There have been a few studies that have examined the change on neurotransmitter substances after brain damage. Numerous neurotransmitters are involved in nervous system function. Acetylcholine is the major mediator of synaptic transmission, and the catecholamines are specialized neurotransmitters of the sympathetic adrenergic system. The catecholamines include norepinephrine, epinephrine, and dopamine. Norepinephrine is the major transmitter agent of the postganglionic sympathetic neurons. Epinephrine is found largely in the adrenal medulla, and its release is associated with the classic fight or flight phenomenon. Dopamine, a precursor of norepinephrine, is present in high concentrations in the caudate nucleus, putamen, and substantia nigra and is, perhaps, best known for its role in the treatment of Parkinson's disease.

The major sources of ascending noradrenergic neurons are the locus ceruleus and lateral tegmental nuclei. These nuclei are likely to be damaged in severe closed head injury in the course of the lesions that affect the rostral midbrain. Noradrenergic neurons do not terminate in conventional synaptic contacts and are likely to be involved in the regulation of synaptic formation and, perhaps, synaptic plasticity (Moore, 1982).

In animals and humans, there is a reduction in catecholamine concentrations in the cerebrospinal fluid following brain damage (Feeney et al., 1982). Several reports have examined specifically traumatic brain injury in humans. A consistent observation is that after the acute stages of the injury, there is a depression of cerebrospinal fluid concentrations of homovanillic acid (HVA), a major metabolite of dopamine, in the cerebrospinal fluid, but not of 5-hydroxyindoleacetic acid (HIAA), a major metabolite of serotonin (van Woerkon, Minderhound, and Nicolai, 1982). These observations have led to speculations that certain pharmacological agents may be useful in rehabilitation efforts. In particular, experimental studies in animals with focal brain lesions have suggested that amphetamines (a group of synthetic adrenergic compounds) may accelerate the recovery of function (Feeney et al., 1982). An anecdotal report of a complicated case suggested a role for the drug dextroamphetamine (Lipper and Tuchman, 1976); however, results of animal studies suggested that the benefit of this and other amphetamines was blocked if the animals were also given haloperidol, a major tranquilizer. Observations in humans with severe head injuries have suggested that L-dopa (dopaminergic precursors) may increase the cerebrospinal fluid HVA concentrations and lead to some clinical improvement (van Woerkon et al., 1982). Unfortunately, the natural evolution of recovery makes the clinical reports of improvement with L-dopa difficult to interpret.

Catecholamines may play a role in the recovery of function. Many of the dopaminergic neurons originate in the mesencephalon, a site of specific injury in severe closed head injury, which may lead to deficits in the attentional system. It is attractive to speculate that dopaminergic or noradrenergic agents, or both, would improve function. Such a model is based on the one used in the treatment of Parkinson's disease, in which dopaminergic precursors (L-Dopa) and agonists (bromocriptine) are used to compensate for the degeneration of dopaminergic neurons. Unfortunately, midbrain lesions are usually markers of a more extensive diffuse axonal injury, and ascending pathways, as well as the termination of these pathways in the forebrain, may also be damaged. Thus, the potential benefits of pharmacotherapy may be lost.

Other drugs have been used in attempts to promote recovery in the closed head injury population. The use of physostigmine has been associated with occasional case reports of clinical improvement (Goldberg, Gratzman, Mattis, et al., 1982; van Woerkon et al., 1982). The rationale for the effectiveness of physostigmine is based either on a nonspecific cholinergic effect on the reticular activating system or on a proposed role of cholinergic systems in memory functions (Drachman and Leavitt, 1974). Positive results have been reported with sporadic cases. Vasopressin has also been tried, and in a recent placebo-controlled study was shown to have no effect in traumatic brain injury (Reichert and Blass, 1982).

To summarize, there is insufficient evidence to fully assess the potential role of certain neurotransmitter substances in the recovery of cognitive function. There is some evidence to suggest that noradrenergic agents may be of benefit. Cholinergic agents have also been suggested, but even less data are available with traumatic brain injury subjects. Finally, although major tranquilizers are the drugs of choice in the early drug management of agitation, caution is advised.

Chapter 4

Neurobehavioral Sequelae

Two classes of neurobehavioral sequelae occur as a result of discrete, focal or widespread, diffuse brain lesions caused by closed head injury. For example, aphasia is a linguistic disorder typically caused by focal brain lesions in the left hemisphere. The neurobehavioral sequelae of diffuse lesions include information processing deficits, generalized cognitive deficits, or neurophysiological deficits, such as attentional disorders, that affect the ability to communicate, but not language per se. Therefore, language and communication problems can result following closed head trauma.

SEQUELAE TYPICAL OF DISCRETE, FOCAL BRAIN LESIONS

Clinicians working with closed head injured patients should be concerned with the identification of disorders most typical of focal lesions in addition to the general cognitive processing deficits most characteristic of closed head injured patients. Thus, diagnostic batteries should provide for at least a screening of the patient's speech, fluency, voice, swallowing ability, visual processing (neglect, discrimination, organization, and so forth), and language. Specific deficits are often difficult to identify as they can be masked by severe cognitive deficits. The treatment of deficits most typical of localized lesions will not be covered since the primary purpose of this textbook is to address the treatment of cognitive problems resulting from diffuse lesions most often sustained following closed head trauma. When specific deficits occur, treatment methods typically used with stroke patients should be considered with adaptations to compensate for levels of cognitive functioning.

Language

Aphasic disorders in the traditional sense are encountered in closed head trauma patients with appropriate focal lesions (Goodglass and Kaplan, 1972). Language disturbances following closed head trauma are usually associated with reduced word fluency, impaired visual naming, impaired auditory comprehension of complex oral commands, anomia, verbal paraphasias, and associated impairments of reading and writing (Heilman, Safran, and Geschwind, 1971a; Levin, 1981; Levin, Grossman, and Kelly, 1976; Sarno, 1980).

Several investigators have indicated that the language disturbance of head injured patients most closely resembles Wernicke's aphasia (Heilman, Safran, and Geschwind, 1971a; Heilman, Watson and Schulman, 1971b; Waterhouse and Fein, 1982). Rather than fit head injured patients into existing systems typically used to classify aphasic patients, Sarno (1980) invented the term "subclinical aphasia" to describe one of three patterns of deficits exhibited by head injured patients. The other two patterns she described were aphasia and subclinical aphasia with dysarthria. Of the head injured patients Sarno studied, 39 per cent showed fluent aphasia, 38 percent demonstrated nonfluent aphasia, 11 per cent were anomic, and 11 percent were globally aphasic.

Thomsen (1976) reported that that pattern of recovery exhibited by the head injured subjects shifted from global to sensory aphasia, finally resolving as amnestic aphasia with word finding deficits.

Levin, Grossman, Sarwar, and Meyers (1981) conducted a longitudinal study of severely injured closed head trauma patients with acute aphasia. Of 12 patients with residual language deficits, 6 showed specific language deficits and 6 had language deficits secondary to more general cognitive disturbances. The patients who fully recovered from aphasia or who exhibited a specific language deficit were within average ranges on the Weschler Adult Intelligence Scale (WAIS). Patients with generalized language deficits had intellectual deficits on the verbal and performance subtest of the WAIS.

Groher (1977) found that all closed head trauma subjects showed marked anomia, characterized by literal and verbal paraphasias initially; however, by the fourth month following injury, confrontation naming was normal for all subjects. Heilman and co-workers (1971a) suggested that typical types of anomic errors include semantic approximations, circumlocutions (e.g. "to make music" for pedals) of a piano) and concrete representations (e.g. "balloon" for circle).

Speech

Levin (1981) suggested that articulation and fluency problems that tend to occur following closed head trauma include stuttering, mutism, echolalia, palilalia, dysarthria, and transient mutism. Helm, Butler, and Benson (1977) believed that acquired stuttering often occurred following closed head injury owing to the bilateral injuries that tend to result. Astrom and colleagues (1980) also found that closed head injured patients exhibited a stuttering or hesitant speech with paraphasias and decreased rate of speaking. It was suggested, however, that these problems were not disabling except in professional workers, speakers, or writers.

Mackay (1982) suggested that speech deficits secondary to closed head trauma can be primarily attributed to specific patterns of residual brain damage, including athetoid pseudobulbar dysfunction with severe bilateral pyramidal damage resulting in severe physical disability with good personality and intellectual functioning and brain stem dysfunction in which asymmetrical cerebellar and pyramidal lesions result throughout the brain stem and cause hemiparetic dysfunction. Piller and Gordon (1981) suggested that neuromotor disorders following closed head trauma are not different from those associated with brain damage from other causes. These authors suggested that spastic states are usual, ataxia is common, and "Parkinson-like" states with various patterns of tremor and rigidity are all seen in closed head trauma patients.

Due to decreased self-monitoring, secondary to cognitive deficits, head injured patients may also exhibit abnormally rapid rates of speaking.

The prosthodontist is an important team member with severely dysarthric patients because palatal lifts are often appropriate. The prosthodontist also provides other oral and facial prostheses when facial injuries accompany closed head trauma.

Nonvocal communication devices can play a crucial part in the rehabilitation of closed head injured patients. It is often necessary to construct special devices that accommodate physical and cognitive limitations specific to individual patients. However, a variety of commercially made devices are available.

Voice

Voice problems can occur secondary to closed head trauma ranging from vocal fold irritation caused by intubation to bilateral vocal fold paralysis. Voice characteristics should be examined. If hoarseness persists following intubation, an otolaryngologist should be consulted as granulomas or other pathological lesions may result. Disorders of volume, especially speaking too loudly, often occur due to inadequate self-monitoring.

Hearing

Cranial nerves that are particularly susceptible to injury following basal skull fractures are the olfactory, oculomotor, and branches of the trigeminal, facial, and auditory nerves. Injury to the eighth cranial nerve or the auditory nerve can cause loss of hearing or dizziness immediately after injury. Deafness due to nerve injury should be distinguished from that caused by the rupture of an eardrum or the presence of blood in the middle ear. The dizziness or vertigo should be distinguished from posttraumatic giddiness.

SEQUELAE TYPICAL OF WIDESPREAD, DIFFUSE BRAIN LESIONS

Diffuse brain lesions secondary to closed head trauma can result in information processing difficulties, cognitive deficits, and neurophysiological disorders.

Information processing difficulties secondary to closed head trauma interfere with an individual's ability to perceive, discriminate, organize, recall, and solve problems using good judgment.

Generalized cognitive breakdowns result in an individual's inability to deal with cognitive constructs at or beyond a specific level of difficulty. An example was provided by Muma (1978), who suggested that the description of item difficulty is a more complex cognitive task than the description of item similarities. When describing differences, Muma indicated that an individual must mentally list the critical elements of one item to which the others are compared in a process of elimination. Description of item similarities on the other hand requires the listing of the critical elements of both items followed by the selection of the similar items from each list as illustrated in Figure 4-1.

Another example of cognitive tasks with varying levels of difficulty was provided by Clark (1973b), who suggested that comprehension of physical space terms, such as "long stick," is cognitively less complex and must be acquired prior to the comprehension of temporal space terms, such as "it took a long time."

Neurobehavioral disorders are characterized by difficulties with attention and recall that can lead to disorientation, disorganization, confusion, and bizarreness or confabulation. Attentional skills required for communication include initiation, as in alerting; sustaining attention; shifting focus of attention; and inhibiting an inappropriate shifting of attention. Behavioral deficits that result from attentional difficulties include perseveration or the inability to appropriately shift the focus of attention, disinhibition, distractibility and impulsivity due to the inability to appropriately inhibit the shifting of the focus

Figure 4-1. Mental processing required for determination of similarities and differences. From Muma, J.R., *Language Handbook: Concepts Assessment and Intervention.* Englewood Cliffs, N.J., Prentice-Hall, 1978. Reprinted with permission.

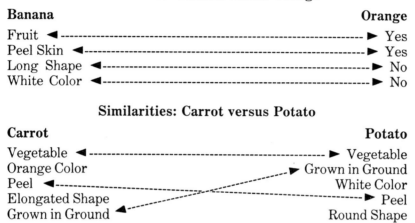

Differences: Banana versus Orange

Banana		Orange
Fruit ◄--►		Yes
Peel Skin ◄--►		Yes
Long Shape ◄--►		No
White Color ◄---►		No

Similarities: Carrot versus Potato

Carrot		Potato
Vegetable ◄--►		Vegetable
Orange Color		Grown in Ground
Peel ◄--------		White Color
Elongated Shape		Peel
Grown in Ground ◄--		Round Shape

of attention, and stimulus boundedness, in which an individual responds to some salient property of the stimulus and fails to remain oriented to the task.

COMMUNICATION DISTURBANCE: LINGUISTIC OR NONLINGUISTIC

Although head trauma patients often do not have linguistic disturbances identical to those experienced by patients with focal left hemisphere lesions, their ability to communicate effectively is certainly impaired. The relationship of language and cognition or thought is not a new topic. Over the past 50 years, many investigators have emphasized the importance of language in forming and shaping thought. Bates (1976) suggested that recent research in the area of pragmatics in children's language is founded on the philosophy of meaning or cognitive thought processing, not specific linguistic structures. Cognition is defined as the mental process or faculty by which knowledge is acquired (*American Heritage Dictionary of the English Language,* 1982). How language and cognition are related is a point of theoretical difference. Cognitive development is described as the development of thought (Vygotsky, 1978); concept attainment (Bruner, Goodnow, and Austin, 1956); and intelligence (Piaget and Inhelder, 1969). Language is the use of symbols usually specific to a particular group, both expressively and receptively, to communicate thoughts and feelings. Some investigators believe that language determines one's thoughts and cognitions. Others think that thoughts and cognitions determine the development and utilization of language. Bloom (1970), probably says it best when she describes linguistic competence as the overlapping of cognition, perception, development, nonlinguistic experience, and linguistic experience.

Bruner (1975) states that all abstract thinking, whether verbal or spatial, requires language as the base. An example of this is the Sapir-Whorf hypothesis, which suggests that the language an individual speaks directly determines major aspects of thought, such as time. A language that codes verbs into tenses objectifies time as if it were a ribbon with various spaces marked off. By contrast, some American Indian languages, such as Hopi, do not use tenses so the peoples speaking these languages have very different concepts of time or duration. Another example is that young children name their drawings only after they have completed them; they need to see them before they can decide what they are. Older children know in advance what they are going to draw. This suggests that, initially, speech follows actions and is provided by and dominated by activity. However, later on speech guides, determines, and dominates the course of action; therefore, the planning function of speech comes into being (Vygotsky, 1978). Bruner, Oliver, and Greenfield (1966) suggested that properties of the cognitive system, such as those of hierarchy and transformations, are first used and perfected within language and only gradually are transferred into thinking in general. Bruner and colleagues claimed that language plays an organizing role in the development of mental operations. They suggested that the acquisition of operative structures is a function of the knowledge of relevant lexical terms.

On the other hand, Piaget (1962) stressed that the developing logical system and the content of thought provide the motives or force for the development of language. Language is regarded as the symbol system for the representation of thought, which develops out of the more general capacity for all functioning along with other types of symbolic representations, such as imagery. Generally, the purpose of language is thought to symbolically represent developed operational cognitive structures. Nelson (1973) suggested that a child forms concepts prior to language learning via four steps: (1) identification of an object as an object; (2) identification of important relationships, usually based on function; (3) identification of new concepts by noting similar, stable, and salient characteristics; and (4) attaching a name or word to a concept such that a word has meaning in the concept that it represents.

Bloom (1970) suggested that language and thought first developed in parallel but merged in early childhood. Bruner (1964) further explains this by postulating that during the first stages, language is dependent on cognitive states. Later on, children use language to activate cognitive processing if a child is developmentally ready. If terms are acquired earlier than their related cognitive system, the terms lack meaning and are usually used in inappropriate ways.

A final theory is that language can be regarded as cognitive process in that both language and thought are said to be defined by logical structure to which models may be applied (Berlin, 1975).

Cognitive functioning is often assessed via linguistic channels, and tasks used to treat specific linguistic deficits can often be used to treat more general cognitive deficits. Normal children speak about what they are doing with speech and action functioning together toward the solution of problem at hand. The more complex the action, the less direct the solution and the greater the importance played by speech in the operation of the whole, such that if the children are not allowed to use speech, they often cannot accomplish the task. Children tend to solve practical tasks with the help of speech as well as eyes and hands. The successful clinician should utilize linguistic skills (verbal, reading, writing, and understanding) and more general cognitive skills in treatment tasks presented to closed head injured patients. However, clinicians must often work on more basic cognitive functions, such as attention, orientation, and memory prior to working on higher level linguistic tasks.

Holland (1982) reviewed similarities and differences of aphasia secondary to focal lesions and language disturbances secondary to closed head trauma. With regard to similarities, it was suggested that both lesion types resulted in anomia and both were characterized auditory comprehension deficits, which tend to improve first, but which persisted for long periods; associated reading and writing deficits; spontaneous recovery periods; and sudden onset. Specific differences included the following: in addition to the naming errors demonstrated by the aphasic individuals, head injured persons substitute names of items related to their personal situation and confabulate; have more difficulty with language use or language pragmatics than do aphasic patients; and have deteriorated communicative competence due to cognitive memory and psychiatric disorders with unaffected language. However, the aphasic patient has specific language deficits. Holland stressed that although language *and* communication problems exist in the head injured person, methods of treatment should differ from those used with aphasic patients owing to qualitative differences between the responses of these two groups.

ASSOCIATED BEHAVIORS

A number of behaviors are associated with closed head trauma that can interfere with treatment programs. These behaviors include (1) personality changes resulting in increased irritability; (2) anxiety and frustration; (3) reduced self-esteem and self-confidence; (4) hyperactivity; (5) impulsivity; (6) egocentricity; (7) emotional liability; (8) inappropriate social judgment; (9) fluctuating moods; (10) hypersexuality; (11) lack of insight; (12) denial of physical and mental limitations; (13) literal interpretations of environmental situations; (14) confusion; (15) confabulation; (16) perseveration; (17) stimulus boundedness; (18) decreased initiation; (19) impaired visual processing skills; (20) fatigue; (21) general mental slowing; (22) low tolerance for visual and auditory extraneous stimuli; (23) motor control difficulties; and (24) amnesia (anterograde, retrograde, and paramnesia).

Following closed head injury, memory disturbances are generally long-lasting and patients are often left with permanent memory deficits of varying degrees for which they must learn to compensate. Various amnesias also frequently occur following closed head injury extending over periods of minutes, hours, days, weeks, or months. Retrograde amnesia refers to a loss of recall of events preceding the injury. Anterograde amnesia or posttraumatic amnesia refers to a loss of recall of events following the injury even though the person is conscious. During recovery, events are gradually recalled in a somewhat orderly fashion, with events occurring close to the injury being recalled last (Astrom et al., 1980; Goodglass and Kaplan, 1979).

Paramnesia refers to a memory disturbance in which locations and people are substituted. For example, the patient might think that the hospital is a hotel. The doctors, therefore, are thought to be bellboys and the nurses are thought to be maids.

Jennett and co-workers (1981) estimated that 70 per cent of head injured patients experience personality changes. Many of the behaviors associated with head trauma, including agitation, withdrawal, and similar traits can be due to amplified premorbid personality traits or the actual head injury; they may also be an expected phase in the recovery process. Quite often, as patients recover to the point that they are aware of their deficits, they become frustrated and subsequently agitated. During this time some patients will strike out at those in their immediate environments. Moods can change from euphoria to depression, followed by outbursts of rage in a relatively short time interval.

Lack of insight and denial of physical and mental limitations can persist for long periods, sometimes years, following closed head trauma. This results in poor planning of short- and long-term events, unrealistic and inappropriate goal setting, and unconcern regarding the future.

Chapter 5

Theoretical Considerations: Information Processing Theories

Three general theories of learning are summarized in chapters that follow, including information processing theories, cognitive theories, and neurophysiological theories. These theories were considered during the preparation of the diagnostic and therapeutic procedures for closed head injured individuals, which are discussed in later chapters. The division between the three theories is artificial, as there are areas of overlap between them. For example, explanations for several specific mental processes, including attention and memory, are offered as components of all three theories.

Most available research regarding the efficacy of training procedures to improve information processing abilities and cognitive skills has been conducted with children. Even within the pediatric population, theoretical issues exist in the comparison of therapeutic techniques used with children with behavioral disorders, learning disabilities, or educable retardation. Other controversies in the pediatric population alone include (1) whether learning disabilities reflect a delay in development or constitute a difference in cognitive processing; (2) the feasibility of developing different models or applying available models of expected development to describe the development of children with learning disabilities; and (3) the application of information processing models to describe the behavior of children with learning disabilities (Parrill-Burnstein, 1981). Head injured patients reportedly have deficits that are both similar and different from the information processing and cognitive deficits experienced by children (Adamovich and Henderson, 1982); however, the effect of neurological insult due to trauma on information processing and cognition requires further investigation. Cognitive breakdowns of normal and learning disabled children, as well as research regarding successful methods of rehabilitating these breakdowns, will be described to serve as a starting point for work with the closed head injured population. Again, the need is stressed for research to determine the appropriateness of utilizing therapy techniques found to be successful in rehabilitating children with closed head injured patients. As we move into a relatively new field, it is the responsibility of each clinician undertaking the challenge of helping to restore the mental processes of closed head trauma patients, to gather data, and to determine the efficacy of their treatment procedures with this population.

GENERAL PRINCIPLES

Quite often, closed head injured patients lack the skills necessary to process and give order to information. This results in difficulty in interacting with the environment and learning from it (Parrill-Burnstein, 1981). Additional difficulty occurs because of an inability to assimilate and accommodate new information. Assimilation refers to the interpretation of objects and events according to a person's current way of thinking or past experiences. Accommodation refers to the revision of concepts and opinions based on new experiences.

Information processing refers to the analysis and synthesis of information in sequential steps (Neisser, 1976). Nebes (1974) suggests that there are two broad modes of processing information, one verbal and the other nonverbal (spatial or visuoconstructive), which are associated respectively with left and right cerebral hemispheres. Many investigators studying hemispheric specialization, including Galin (1974), Bever (1975), and Gazzaniga (1979), have suggested that the two hemispheres are specialized for different cognitive styles in such a way that the right hemisphere processes information in a more holistic, gestalt, or simultaneous fashion whereas the left hemisphere, is responsible for more analytical, linear, or sequential processing. Language is often identified with serial information processing typical of the left hemisphere, and spatial representations are usually identified with parallel or simultaneous information processing typical of the right hemisphere. However, as a result of their work with split brain patients, Zaidel and Sperry (1977) and Gazzaniga and Hillyard (1971) suggested that the right hemisphere is adept at language processing or sequential processing if it has enough time to explore the nature of the stimulus. Kirby (1980) suggested that (1) simultaneous processing takes place in both cerebral hemispheres, with involvement of the parieto-occipital areas in verbal and nonverbal tasks; (2) successive processing take place in the fronto-temporal areas of both hemispheres; and (3) the prefrontal lobes of both hemispheres are considered to be responsible for the planning and programming of behavior after incoming information is analyzed.

Kirby (1980) pointed out that both types of processing, perhaps in different proportions, are required in both verbal and nonverbal tasks. Individuals seem to vary in their abilities to use simultaneous or successive processing; however, the effectiveness of an individual's performance is often dependent on the ability to utilize both types and to select the appropriate mode given a specific situation.

Although information regarding hemispheric asymmetries can be traced to the nineteenth century, a great deal of research occured in this area in the 1960s (Springer and Deutsch, 1981). Methods utilized to investigate brain asymmetries include studies of patients with left or right hemisphere brain damage, commissurotomies, or hemispherectomies, and normal subjects. Investigations designed to answer the same questions have often produced conflicting results or have suggested speculations or conclusions that are not data-based (Springer and Deutsch, 1981). In addition to clinical observations of specifically designed tasks, scientific techniques utilized in hemispheric specialization investigations include direct electrical stimulation of the hemispheres (Penfield and Roberts, 1959); the Wada Test (Wada and Rasmussen, 1960); patching of one eye (Myers, 1956); tachistoscopic stimulus presentation (Bryden and Rainey, 1963); dichotic listening tasks (Kimura, (1961); naming of items that subjects feel with their hands but do not see (Gazzaniga and Hillyard, 1971); use of a Z lens developed by Zaidel (1975); chimeric figures (Levy, Trevarthen, and Sperry, 1972); lateral eye movements (Kinsbourne, 1972); electroencephalography (EEG) (Galin and Ornstein, 1972); evoked potentials (Buschbaum and Fedio, 1970); blood flow (Risberg, Halsey, Wells and Wilson, 1975); cerebral metabolism (Plum, Gjedde, and Samson, 1976); and computed tomography (CT scan) (LeMay and Geschwind, 1978).

Information processing theorists suggest various levels of information processing, following the initial analytical or holistic processing of verbal and nonverbal information, which are necessary for information to be learned or to become meaningful. Information processing theorists regard humans as analogous to complex machines, such as computers, with elaborate programs that enable individuals to deal with information (Flavell and Wellman, 1977). A human being is considered to be an active processor of information with certain processing limitations.

The levels of sensory, perceptual, and cognitive analyses imply a hierarchy of stages through which incoming information can progress in order to be remembered. Atkinson and Shiffrin (1968) hypothesized that information analysis is sequential rather than hierarchical, involving the moving of information from one memory store to another. In their theory, sensory information is registered or perceived. If further analyzed, the sensory information takes on meaning, primarily verbal, and progresses to the short-term memory store. To enter the long-term memory store, the information in the short-term memory store is further analyzed, organized, and rehearsed.

Parrill-Burnstein's information processing model of problem solving (1981) is presented in Figure 5-1.

Information processing during problem solving involves several stages, including reception, perception, discrimination, organization, and memory, before an individual can generate a solution to a problem, evaluate that solution using feedback or results, and generate a new solution if indicated. Breakdown at any stage can result in an inability to solve a problem. These stages of information processing will be described in the following section.

Reception

Reception is the process by which physical information is received by the sense organs. Initial arousal or alerting depends on the strength of the visual, auditory, verbal, tactile, olfactory, gustatory, or vestibular stimulus.

Perception

Perception is the integration and interpretation of information received at the sense organs based on an internal or stored representation of the stimulus. Perception is not a complex set of discriminations; instead, it is based upon categorization or classification abilities. People perceive according to how they classify or represent experiences based on prior knowledge (Kirby and Biggs, 1980; Shaw and Cutting, 1980). Perception can be sometimes at odds with physical measures because the two systems of meaning do not have common bases, and structures perceived in one context may appear different from the same structures

Figure 5-1. Information processing model of problem solving. From Parrill-Burnstein, M. *Problem solving and learning disabilities: An information processing approach.* New York: Grune & Stratton, 1981. Reprinted with permission.

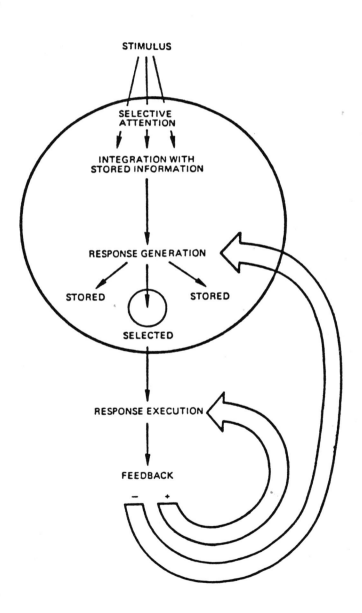

perceived in another context, such as the famous Müller-Lyer figures, in which two lines of equal length appear unequal when angles of different degrees are attached–for example, ⟩⟨ ↕. According to Broadbent (1958), irrelevant information is filtered out at multiple levels of processing. Broadbent suggests that the perceiver is limited in the capacity to process all peripherally available information; however, Neisser (1976) proposes that unwanted information is not filtered out. Instead, he suggests that this information is simply not attended to. Selection is regarded as a positive process, internal to the organism, which is manifested in covert behavior. Stereotypes also direct the process of a person's perception by biasing the way he or she sees and interprets someone's behavior or events (Bower, 1978). The relationship of the speaker and his or her environment in a particular situation also colors that individual's perceptions. Other aspects affecting perception that might interfere with a linear covariance between psychological and physiological parameters include biological, psychological, and socioculture levels of analysis (Bellugi and Studdert-Kennedy, 1980).

Perception requires several levels of processing, including the analysis of physical and sensory features–i.e., brightness, pitch, and so forth–followed by a matching of that input with past learning, resulting in pattern recognition and meaning extraction. Finally, elaboration occurs in which the stimulus triggers images and associations. During encoding, the subject codes material at a suboptimal level based on information contained in long-term memory, followed by elaboration in which the subject sees some personal relevances he or she had not noticed before, which relates this new material to previous material resulting in a higher level stored version (Craik and Lockhart, 1972).

Discrimination

Discrimination is the ability to differentiate two or more stimuli using selective attention. Individuals must discriminate multiple aspects of a stimulus situation at any moment in time. Irrelevant and extraneous stimuli must be determined based on contextual cues. The salient or pertinent aspects of items, therefore, are context dependent and are not necessarily determined by the strength or intensity of the stimulus (e.g., loudness, brightness), as would generally be the case during reception. The threshold for highly pertinent information must be adjusted continually using a cognitive rather than sensory process, which evaluates existing inputs and expectations of future inputs.

Organization

According to Piaget (1963, 1966, 1969; Piaget and Inhelder, 1969), organized structures emerge from experience as a result of two innate processes: (1) the ability to organize or integrate information into systematic forms; and (2) the ability to adapt information by assimilating or altering information to fit existing structures as well as by accommodating or changing existing structures to reorganize information. Organization plays an important role in the acquisition of new information, in recall, and in other higher level processes, such as problem solving and reasoning. Categorization of information requires reasoning according to fixed rules, which must be learned. To solve problems, each discrete action or component of the solution must be sequenced according to the priority of each component. Head trauma patients have particular difficulty with organized thinking, which results in difficulty in learning new information and in retrieving information previously learned.

Memory

During information processing, past memories are required for encoding, assimilating, and accommodating information. Memory allows for progression through the various levels of the problem-solving process, and it is essential for generating responses and responding appropriately following feedback. Additionally, the more information to be processed, the greater the load on memory (Parrill-Burnstein, 1981). Strategies to reduce the load on working memory are learned as a child develops. For example, when asked to identify rods of various lengths and thicknesses, adults formed a mental checklist of all of the variables to be controlled and then searched for rods that met all of the appropriate dimensional criteria at once. When children performed this task, they took their cues from the perceptual comparisons of one rod to the next, rather than using a mental checklist – for example, instead of looking for a long rod that was brass, thin, and round, they first looked for a rod which was long and similar in global appearance with the short rod they had just selected, initially dealing only with the aspects long and short. After finding a long rod, they compared its charateristics to the short rod one by one, taking their cue from a conceptual comparison rather than a mental checklist (Kirby and Biggs, 1980).

As the number of stimuli increase, the cognitive demands with regard to the amount of attention and memory necessary to order and evaluate the concepts simultaneously also increase.

Halford (1980) suggested that a minimum information processing capacity of four chunks of information would be required to deal with two stimuli as these two bits of information would have to be matched with two environmental or internal sources. Processing three stimuli would require an information processing capacity of six chunks of information to allow for the matching of these three stimuli to three additional stimuli. The ability to solve more complex problems requires an increased information processng capacity (Kirby and Biggs, 1980). As a person is able to deal with larger amounts of information, the individual chunks of information are actually grouped – that is, two, three, or more chunks of information are grouped to form a separate chunk, allowing the subject to deal with greater amounts of information. Immature thinking processes of earlier stages can be due to limitations caused by limited working memory. As the subject retrieves one piece of data, another piece is forced out of the working memory. Therefore, a person will never have all the information he or she needs to solve the problem in the working space at the same time (Kirby and Biggs, 1980). Clinicians must consider each patient's level of information processing and the load placed on working memory during the preparation of all therapy tasks.

In early social development, there are two different types of memory. One is natural memory, which is characterized by a nonmediated impression of materials such that information returned is what is immediately perceived. Later in social development, when simple operations – such as tying a knot or marking a stick as a reminder – are used to facilitate memory, the operational memory is extended beyond the biological dimensions through the incorporation of artificial or self-generated stimuli. The use of artificial stimuli or signs is unique to human beings and is absent even in highest species of animals (Vygotsky, 1978).

Norman (1968) suggests three different stages of memory processing: (1) an attention mechanism selects among various sources of sensory information only after they have activated their representation in storage. The process of choosing among sources is, therefore, combined with the process of interpreting each input; (2) a storage system may be activated temporarily (short-term or primary memory); and (3) retrieval occurs through repeated queries of the storage system until satisfactory output is obtained. Atkinson and Shiffrin (1968) suggested that memory proceeds in orderly fashion from input to storage in a few seconds, leading from an attentional phase, which moves memory into a short-term storage system for approximately 17 seconds, in which information is organized to be stored in long-term memory.

Memory comprises three basic components: encoding, storage, and retrieval. Encoding refers to the acquisition of information. The encoding of a modeled behavioral sequence into memory involves two symbolic representational systems, a verbal representation and a sensory image. Neisser (1976) referred to echoic memory and oconic memory, which represent an initial or primary auditory or visual sensory storage, respectively. Marshall and Newcombe (1980) referred to semantic versus episodic memory. Semantic memory is recall of knowledge organized according to the meanings of symbols, concepts, and relationships. Episodic memory is recall of temporally ordered events and spatial relationships. These authors reported striking disociations between semantic and episodic memory as well as short- and long-term memory. Korsakoff patients were found to have intact semantic memory such that their conversations were grammatically intact despite grossly impaired episodic memory (Bellugi and Studdert-Kennedy, 1980). Retrieval is of three types: recognition, cued recall, and free recall. Recognition occurs in the presence of the object or event. Cued recall occurs in the presence of a part or an association of the object or event. Free recall occurs in the absence of the object or event. (Parrill-Burnstein, 1981).

During recall, the position of information in a list of information presented can interfere with the recall of that information. Retention of items presented at the beginning of the list is referred to as a primacy effect. A primacy effect indicates active rehearsal of the initial items, which is a strategy that increases in use with age (Flavell, 1970). Items presented last in the list do not require rehearsal because their retention is not interfered with by the presentation of additional items. The recall of final items is called a recency effect.

When an item is present in primary store, incorporation into secondary storage becomes more difficult as later items divert the attention of the organization process from the prior input and also divert the energies of the mechanism that prolongs the active memory trace. This is a form of retroactive interference. Proactive interference refers to the interference caused by items presented prior to the stimulus that is to be recalled. Items that are homogeneous or that closely resemble the material to be recalled tend to cause the greatest interference.

Two theories of memory accounting for the recall of temporally sequenced stimuli include the association theory and the description theory. Proponents of the association theory propose that we do not store individual items but instead store the associations that relate them to one another. If insufficient associations are made during storage, certain inputs will not lead to recall of the information stored. If too many associations exist, "noise" results because every input query can retrieve every item of information, and the system might as well be a completely disorganized, random selective device (Norman, 1968). Two important aspects of items to be retrieved are their discriminability and their constructibility – that is, how well they discriminate among all possible memory records and how well they can be constructed at the time retrieval is required (Norman, 1979).

Proponents of the description theory suggest that the description of an entity that an individual is trying to recall is a collection of perspectives, each of which is the way of viewing that entity in terms of a previously known prototype (Norman, 1979). The description of an item to be recalled must uniquely specify the original encoding. If information was encoded from one perspective at the time of acquisition but described using a different perspective at the time of retrieval, the process of retrieval would fail because the retrieval specifications lead to inappropriate descriptions and inappropriate evaluations.

Geschwind (1982) proposes two types of defects in distant or recent memory, including (1) a disconnection in which stored material is simply unavailable to be read out of a memory bank; or (2) a storage defect in which there is an actual loss of the memory trace. The patient who lost a trace would not be aided by cues (Patten, 1982). Memory retrieval depends upon the formation of a description of the information sought, and success or failure of a retrieval attempt depends upon the ability to decode information at the time retrieval is desired. Errors often reflect the retrieval failure rather than loss from storage or a retention failure (Norman, 1979).

Flavell and Wellman (1977) discuss the development of metamemory. Metamemory is a term coined by Flavell to describe an individual's knowledge of awareness of memory processes (e.g., storage and retrieval strategies). Metamemory increases with age and is helpful in preparing for future retrieval (Parrill-Burnstein, 1981). Lawson's description (1980) of metamemory-metacognition is presented in Figure 5-2.

Reasoning and Problem Solving

During problem solving, individuals generate response options

Figure 5-2. Metacognition as part of an information-processing system. From Lawson, M.J. Metamemory: Making decisions about strategies. In J.R. Kirby and J.B. Biggs, *Cognition development and instruction.* New York, Academic Press, 1980. Reprinted with permission.

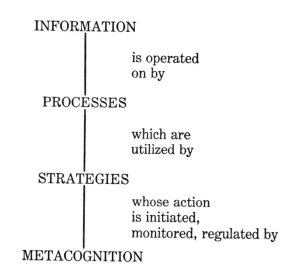

INFORMATION

            is operated
            on by

PROCESSES

            which are
            utilized by

STRATEGIES

            whose action
            is initiated,
            monitored, regulated by

METACOGNITION

based on relevant information. Once a solution to a problem is deduced, it must be then checked both against knowledge of reality and against reality itself. Hypothesis testing requires the following problem-solving analyses: stimulus differentiation, selective attention, response generation, response execution, and response to feedback (Parrill-Burnstein, 1978).

Piaget (1969) reported that a child's problem-solving ability is limited by his or her level of cognitive functioning such that he or she can conceptually distort what is observed or cannot recognize the need to verify a response depending on specific levels of cognitive ability. If a consistent match is not possible during hypothesis checking following the generation of a solution to a problem, the system may decide that the problem is unsolvable; however, in real-life situations this is not acceptable. Therefore, the system must make the most consistent matching that it can in order to permit the deduction of the solution to the problem (Kirby and Biggs, 1980). Quite often, head trauma patients feel comfortable saying there is no solution rather than going the one step farther and coming up with the most consistent match when identical matching is not possible. Other breakdowns during problem solving might be due to more primary difficulties, such as an inability to identify salient features, a deficient short-term memory store, or an inability to recognize associations of stimuli.

RESEARCH: SPECIFIC THERAPY IMPLICATIONS
General Information Processing

Kirby (1980) suggested four types of instructional approaches to facilitate information processing. These approaches are summarized in Table 5-1.

Parrill-Burnstein (1981) suggested that remediation of information processing problems should include the following: (1) segmentation of work periods; (2) use of training techniques to focus attention and facilitate rehearsal; (3) avoidance of the presentation of competing cues with relevant information; and (4) use of instructions to increase self-monitoring skills.

She suggested that performances of children would be improved if children were given intermittent breaks, changes in the response required, limitation of input in terms of length and complexity, and changes in the type of tasks assigned. Younger children with learning disabilities responded more appropriately following positive reinforcement and through instruction that successfully integrated available stimulus information and improved recognition memory. This investigator also reported that learning disabled children had difficulty during social interactions in which more than one person was speaking at once. To deal with this, it was suggested that mock situations be set up in classrooms in which children are advised of social cues, such as loudness of the message, proximity of the speaker, and the relative importance of the speaker of the message. A final recommendation was the use of a stop watch to modify latency and accuracy. Microcomputer programs are also available to accomplish this.

In order to achieve generalization, Meichenbaum (1980) suggested the following: (1) feedback must be meaningful and explicit; (2) multiple stimuli should be used; (3) direct instructions to generalize the strategy to certain types of tasks should be specified; and (4) general strategies should be given to supplement specific strategies that are to be taught.

Table 5-1. Instructional Approaches to Facilitate Information Processing

Source of problem			
1.	Block 1 Arousal	Impulsivity Hyperactivity Inattentiveness	Teach scanning strategies Teach verbal self-control Overlearning and coding? Biofeedback?
2.	Block 2 Processing	Specific learning problems	Train the actual processes, if they are mutable and not culturally valued
3.	Block 3 Processing	Specific learning problems	Exploit processing strengths through curriculum design
4.	Block 4	Disorganization	Teach strategies, when to use which processes
	Planning	Retardation	Teach "learning to learn," analytic approaches, overlearn particular plans

Some investigators have reported success in teaching children self-control strategies. Egeland (1974) was successful in teaching strategies for scanning visual displays with learning disabled children. Luria (1961) successfully taught verbal self-control strategies aimed at the gradual internalization of the controlled behavior, proceeding from external verbal control by others to overt control by self and finally to covert verbal control of the individual's own behavior. Douglas (1972) was successful with learning disabled children with regard to encouraging the listener to stop, look, and listen as a technique to control impulsivity.

Parrill-Burnstein (1981) studied the use of semantic cues to facilitate encoding in children with learning disabilities. Children were asked to use a sentence to describe the relationship between new vocabulary words, such as cowboy and horse. The children were then asked to recall the word pair without cues. If a child had difficulty, the examiner gave one member of the pair and finally both members of the pair randomly for the child to associate. Children with learning disabilities were found not to use semantic cues to aid their recall. Parrill-Burnstein (1978) taught kindergarten children a focusing strategy. Children who were taught to complete sequences of steps, including the appropriate response to feedback, performed significantly better than children in other training conditions. The children also benefited most when exposed to a strategy that was most consistent with their developmental level.

Herman and Seigel (1978) evaluated the effect of location on layout construction. The effects of closed (city within the classroom) and open (city within the gymnasium) environments were compared. Kindergarten children performed in a significantly different manner depending on the situation. Further analysis indicated that the smaller space seemed to facilitate spatial imagery with youngsters at the kindergarten age. The author suggested that these children had less difficulty forming relationships between objects in a reduced space. When working on spatial imagery with head injured patients, it appears that treatment might be more successful if the clinician presents a reduced space situation first.

Head injured persons frequently exhibit problem-solving difficulties. Parrill-Burnstein and Baker-Ward (1979) found that children with learning disabilities generated significantly fewer hypotheses or options on problem-solving tasks than children without learning problems. Gholson, Levine, and Phillips (1972) identified the strategies used by children and adults to solve hypothesis-testing problems. These included a focusing strategy, a dimension-checking strategy, and an hypothesis-checking strategy. A focusing strategy was the most efficient strategy, enabling the individual to solve the problems in the fewest number of trials. Children and adults who used this strategy processed all available information simultaneously and took into account feedback across the trials. Children using the dimension strategy did not process and evaluate all the available information. Instead, only those cues associated with a specific dimension (e.g., color) were processed and evaluated simultaneously. The hypothesis-checking strategy was the least efficient strategy. Children who used this strategy processed and evaluated cues separately (e.g., red, then green, and so forth). The efficiency of the strategy used was found to increase with age. A number of explanations have been offered to account for differences in the hypothesis-testing behaviors of children. These are mediation (Phillips and Levine, 1975); stimulus differentiation (Gholson and McConville, 1974); selective attention (Offenbach, 1974); memory (Eimas, 1969; 1970); and feedback (Gholson and McConville, 1974; Parrill-Burnstein, 1978).

Memory

Research and therapy implications regarding the facilitation of memory with children, non-brain-injured adults, and neurologically impaired subjects will be reviewed.

Children. Hallahan, Kaufman, and Ball (1974) found that learning disabled children did not recall as much relevant information than did those without learning problems. Incidental recall was similar for both groups. Before the age of eight years, children with learning disabilities did not rehearse spontaneously; however, they could be induced to do so with the result of enhancing recall performance. Presenting items grouped by category (Suiter and Potter, 1978) and providing instructions to improve use of three-dimensional objects (Swanson, 1977a, b) resulted in improved recall.

Bryan (1972) and Parrill-Burnstein (1981) suggested that learning disabled children demonstrated poorer performance than those without learning problems when presented with both verbal and visual items. In addition, verbal stimuli were better recalled than auditory stimuli. No significant effect was obtained for the type of instructions given. Bryan concluded that rehearsal or directing attention did not facilitate recall of the children in the learning disabled groups. However, he studied subjects with a wide range of disabilities.

Case (1974) conducted a study to verify the benefits of his therapeutic program with learning disabled children regarding their control of variables. With this technique, the number of variables with which the child had to deal was gradually expanded, thus controlling the load on memory. Eighty per cent of the subjects showed a comparable degree of mastery of the material, which was higher than that normally attained by untrained eight year olds. There was also no decline in performance when the test was readministered two months later.

Non-Brain Injured Adults. Martin and Caramazza (1982) concluded, following three experiments, that a phoneme code facilitated the retention of verbal items in short-term memory.

Bower (1978) found that teaching older people to use mnemonics aided their otherwise failing memories. Bower also (1980) found that visual imagery facilitated memory in normal adults. Halford (1980) suggested that the use of imagery is not restricted to simple problems. It can be used for any of the most sophisticated and creative thinking.

Neurologically Impaired Patients. Vallier and Wertz (1978) studied eight subjects who experienced right cerebrovascular accidents and 18 subjects who had experienced left cerebrovascular accidents. No significant difference was found between groups in an overall ability to recall previously presented stimuli. The results also revealed no significant difference between groups with regard to the number of errors made in response to the mode of stimulus presentation. Pictorial stimuli were remembered better than auditory or lexical stimuli, and the ability to recall the original stimulus mode was better for pictures than for auditory lexical stimuli.

Adamovich (1978) reported perceptual confusions following an investigation of the short-term memory of aphasic patients with left hemisphere lesions. The 26 letters of the alphabet were presented visually or auditorially (spoken names), followed by an imposed response delay before the subjects identified the letter presented by pointing to the letters on response cards. Aphasic subjects made significantly more errors than did normal controls on all tasks. Adamovich suggested that the aphasic patients differed from the normal control subjects with regard to the type of sensory code used. The control subjects made errors that sounded alike or rhymed with the stimulus letter regardless of input modality. Therefore, even though the letters were presented visually, the normal subjects appeared to use speech to code the information to be recalled. In contrast, the aphasic subjects made errors that sounded like the stimulus when information was presented auditorially, but made errors that resembled the stimulus when information was presented visually. Adamovich indicated that aphasic subjects did not appear to use a speech code to store the names of letters in short-term memory, as did normal subjects.

Patten (1982) indicated that the verbal memory deficit of aphasic individuals is material-specific and is more incapacitating in everyday life than is the visual memory deficit experienced by patients with right hemisphere damage. It was suggested that the paucity of right hemisphere cases referred for memory evaluation is due to the fact that visual memory is relatively nonessential in everyday life, and patients with right hemisphere lesions are satisfied with the preserved verbal memory or are unaware of their visual memory deficits. Patten worked with patients with dominant hemisphere lesions. The patients were required to learn 10 words and related images – for example, tea with the image of a teacup. Patten found that the use of imagery, following a three-stage training program, improved memory performance at acquisition and following a 30 minute period. The facilitative effect of the imagery training, however, was not evident at a one week delay interval.

Brooks (1974) found that digits forward (simple span tasks) were resistant to types of brain damage that usually result in memory disturbances.

Based on investigations of 50 patients with memory problems resulting from right hemisphere damage, left hemisphere damage, and bilateral lesions, Patten (1982) found the following memory deficits: (1) recent memory was worse than remote memory; (2) defects of remote memory were present in over half the patients; (3) if remote memory was impaired, recent memory was always impaired also; (4) the patients with right hemisphere damage did better with verbal memory; (5) the patients with left hemisphere damage did better with visual memory; (6) gustatory and olfactory recent memory was more resistant to brain disease than verbal or visual recall; (7) the dominant hemisphere was responsible for gustatory memory and the nondominant hemisphere for olfactory memory; (8) if gustatory memory was impaired, verbal memory was always impaired also; and (9) in all types of patients, the memory deficits revealed a diassociation between the ability to recall distant events of a personal nature (home, father's name, and so forth), and an inability to recall distant events of an impersonal nature, (for example, the name of the president during World War II).

When memory functions were evaluated after head injury, Fodor (1972) noted two trends. Acute closed head injury patients with approximately normal intelligence, as measured by the Ammons Test, demonstrated a decreased capacity to utilize structure and delayed recall compared with normal control subjects. Patients with low intelligence demonstrated wider memory deficits, which affected perception and immediate recall. Fodor found that closed head injured subjects with normal intelligence did not use organization as an aid in the delayed recall of related stimulus material as effectively as subjects in a normal control group.

Brooks (1974) suggested that errors occurred with a closed head injured group, such that they were unable to identify previously displayed items as familiar. Brooks suggested that this could be due to (1) poor initial learning, so that less material was committed to memory, or (2) the patient's adopting strict criteria, with the identification of items only if they were quite certain of the correct answer.

Adamovich and Henderson (1982) studied 32 closed head injured patients and found that these patients showed poorer recall than did normal control subjects with regard to free recall tasks. Subjects in this study showed no discernible strategy to recall items and tended to provide neologistic words. The normal control group did demonstrate several strategies (e.g., phonemic: pin, pen, pan; semantic: ski, snow, sled) to facilitate recall. Adamovich and Henderson (1984) studied performances during word fluency tasks using quantitative and qualitative measures. Ten closed head injured individuals were included in the investigation: 8 high level, nonfluent aphasic patients with left hemisphere damage, 9 right hemisphere damaged patients, 13 normal subjects younger than age 50, and 12 normal subjects older than age 50. The group with closed head injuries generated more words overall than the group with left cerebrovascular accidents (CVA) and the same number as the group with right CVA, yet they used fewer strategies to generate the words than did both of the latter groups. The closed head injured group used the strategies of identical vowels (e.g., cod, cot) and one-syllable words significantly less often than did the young normal control group. The strategies seen most often in all subject groups involved use of frequently occurring words, one-syllable words, and identical vowels. The closed head trauma subjects changed strategies during the task more often than did all of the other subject groups.

Ben-Yishay (1982) reported that patients experiencing head trauma had difficulty remembering important facts owing to discontinuities in understanding and an inability to continue trying. Craik and Lockhart (1972) found their patients were able to learn and memorize but failed to draw on this information to resolve problems. This was suggested to be due to frontal damage, which causes a lack of incentive. Marshall (1982) reported that the impairment of memory in organic brain disorders especially affects the capacity to form new memories and to recall recent events. Finally, Brooks (1974) reported that the persistence and severity of memory deficits in a sample of severe head injured patients could be attributed to recognition difficulties.

Groher (1977) studied 14 male subjects who had experienced closed head trauma. The Porch Index of Communicative Abilities and the Wechsler Memory Scale were administered one week following regain of consciousness and every 30 days for four months. The results suggested that, initially, the patients had decreased gestural, verbal, and graphic skills, with gestural skills ranking lowest and verbal skills ranking highest. Four months following trauma, graphic skills were superior to verbal and gestural performances. Reading comprehension was poor. On the Wechsler Memory Scale, mental control, logical memory, and digits were within normal limits after the fifth session.

Wetzel and Squire (1982) found that brain injured subjects rapidly improved on all skills measured by the Wechsler Adult Intelligence Scale, with recovery of all skills within six months following injury. Full return of verbal skills measured by this test occurred after 11 weeks following trauma in the majority of patients. Performance skills took longer to return. If duration of post-traumatic amnesia was greater than 11 weeks, these investigations reported little to no restoration of verbal or performance skills.

Yorkston (1981) successfully used relatively intact language skills to compensate for poor sequencing skills with a closed head injured patient. The patient was asked to make up a story about pictures to be sequenced, which was verbalized and read, followed by removal of linquistic cues. This investigator emphasized the need to base treatment decisions on data and suggested the use of logarithmic scales to chart patient progress.

Chapter 6

Theoretical Considerations: Cognitive Theories

GENERAL PRINCIPLES

Cognitive theorists working in the area of normal development have specified difficulty levels of a variety of cognitive tasks or functions. Owing to the current paucity of research, clinicians treating the cognitive dysfunctions of closed head injured patients should consider the findings of cognitive theorists during the evaluation of cognitive functioning and during task selection in cognitive rehabilitation programs, at least as a starting point. Carefully designed research investigations should be conducted to compare normal cognitive development to cognitive breakdown secondary to closed head trauma.

Probably the best known cognitive developmental theorist is Piaget. Piaget (1969) suggested that children develop through stages that are defined by different intellectual requirements and accomplishments. The interaction of current level of cognitive structure and new experiences with an arousal of interest leads to the development of understanding. Piaget suggested that the clinician should be aware of the child's current level of functioning and that treatment should be oriented more toward the individual than group norms, with each child being given considerable control over his or her own learning. According to Piaget, the periods or stages through which children pass are age-related but not age-determined. The cognitive developmental stages proposed by Piaget include the following: (1) the sensorimotor period (birth to age two); (2) the preoperational period (age two to age seven); (3) the concrete operational period (age seven to approximately age 11); and (4) the formal operations period (age 12 to age 16).

During the sensorimotor period, interactions with the environment occur at a motor level. Effective components include physical movements, such as reaching. Initially, no attempt is made to coordinate two or more actions. The subject and object are not clearly differentiated, and situations cannot be evoked that are not actually perceived. Reflexive, manual action that has no relation to the environment leads to actions that result in gratification. Next, actions are related to some consequence in the world. Toward the end of this period, actions can be completed that have two components (e.g., if an object is on a towel, the towel is pulled to obtain the object that is real focus of interest). In general, however, the stimuli must be manipulated. Through motoric involvement, concept learning takes place.

It is said that language builds on the cognitive abilities that are developed in the sensorimotor period, and that this development must occur before language acquisition. Specific required cognitive skills include object permanence, imitation of previously seen actions, and anticipation of future positions of objects. During the sensorimotor stage, the ability to put things in spatial or temporal order develops, as does the ability to classify items as a whole category of objects with the same action. In addition, the person is separated from objects acted on. Toward the end of this period, the ability to develop symbolic representations, including language, deferred imitation, mental imagery, symbolic games, and drawing, is developed.

During the preoperational stage, forms of symbolic behavior appear. Obvious properties, such as height, weight, and length, are focused on, and one concept can be dealt with at a time (such as size, shape, or color). At this stage, difficulty in switching sets occurs. For example, if blocks are first sorted by size, switching to sorting by color would cause difficulty. Egocentric or self-centered behavior is prevalent, and concepts of rules and mental representations are lacking.

During the first part of the preoperational stage, language and other symbolic instruments are attained. Deductive skills are missing, however, which permit the making of logical predictions based on concept extensions beyond the actual perception of a situation. The second half of this period marks the beginning of decentralization and preparations for the development of operations. Gradual dissociation of temporal from spatial actions occurs, and the concept of duration is understood – that is, time is inversely proportional to velocity. The use of feedback begins at this period (i.e., thought is regulated by feedback).

During the concrete operational stage, the first structures appear that show system coherence is sufficient to allow certain logical deductive operations. Inverse operations or reverse objects and elements are possible. The invariances associated with conservation are achieved at this time. The trial-and-error action of the previous stage becomes fused at this level with anticipation, which follows from a closure of a logical structure. Second order symbols, such as numbers, are attained during this period. If read history, a piece of evidence or a fact can be put forward to support a response to a question, yet when forming a judgment, perceptionally dominating evidence is used, resulting in the formation of circumstantial judgments. With some, the judgment may reflect an emotional reaction rather than a cognitive possibility. At the earlier concrete level, one piece of circumstantial evidence is seized to support a simple unqualified judgment. Concepts of time allow freedom from the present and its constraints on space. This, along with the acquisition of reversibility of thought, allows the retracing of time in either direction. Concepts become more abstract and are no longer confined to sensory qualities. Two concepts can be dealt with simultaneously. Operations attain maximum extension and utility through generalization. Generalizations are made too readily on the basis of a few pieces of information, even though the ability to identify and use all of the facts or reasons presented and to see elementary relationships among these facts or events exists. The ability to go beyond data presented to form and test hypotheses is still lacking.

Finally, the formal operational level marks the attainment of all structures required in logical thought, which leads to logical deduction. The formulation of hypotheses and the use of data to test them are possible. Other abilities acquired during this period include the recognition of links between relationships rather than the mere perception of relationships between events, the inference of motives, the ability to provide a comprehensive account of more than one possibility, and delaying making a judgment until all possibilities have been considered.

Bruner's (1964) developmental hierarchical relationship for the emergence or acquisition of cognitive processing systems was based on the following stages: (1) an inactive stage or motoric stage, which corresponds to Piaget's sensorimotor stage. Bruner suggests that in early infancy, learning results from motoric engagement through action patterns; (2) the iconic processing stage or the imagery stage, which involved perceptual or image processing such that the toddler and preschooler process in terms of perceptual attributes, including colors, shapes, size, position, and so forth; (3) the symbolic or representational stage, in which experiences are represented in prototypes or categories based on function. Experiences can be represented with language. Symbolic information is thought to be much easier to store in memory than is iconic information. In summary, Bruner proposed that the dominant form of internal representation in the child progresses from the inactive to the iconic to the symbolic with motorics, visual imagery, and language, respectively, being typical mediums of these modalities. Symbolic representation is thought to dominate adult cognition, with language serving an important role in all of the adult's cognitive activities. Bruner suggested that during initial language development, representations of experience will tend to be iconic rather than symbolic or nonverbal rather than verbal. During this time, a verbal measure of memory, such as the digits span recall, would not be an adequate index to capacities.

Instructional theorists pose theories of learning cognitive processes. It is assumed that simpler skills are acquired and integrated or combined into more complex rules and generalizations. Gagne and Briggs (1979) described categories of learned capabilities, including (1) intellectual skills; (2) cognitive strategies; (3) verbal information; (4) motor skills; and (5) attitudes. The authors suggested that a cognitive strategy is an internally controlled process by which an individual attends, learns, remembers, modifies, and thinks.

Neopiagetian theory, as proposed by Case (1978), bridges the gap between Piaget's theory of learning and educational or instructional theories of learning. Case (1978) suggested the following: (1) teaching should be initiated at the level of development; (2) exercises should be designed that encourage transition from one stage to the next; (3) operational structures that underlie specific tasks should be identified through a structural analysis; (4) assessment of current functioning should occur; (5) this assessment should be followed by the establishment of an instructional design or a sequence of instructions. With neopiagetian methology, cognitive retraining is tuned more finely to the cognitive strategies and resources of the patients themselves.

RESEARCH: SPECIFIC THERAPY IMPLICATIONS

Adamovich and Henderson (1982) studied the type and degree of changes in cognitive functioning that occurred during and following a cognitive retraining program for eight closed head trauma patients. Subjects ranged in age from 17 to 27 years old with a mean of 20 years. Years of education ranged from 11 to 14 years, with a mean of 12.2 years, and time following injury ranged from 2 to 12 weeks, with a mean of 7.5 weeks. The amount of speech-language therapy ranged from 2 to 4 months, with a mean of 2.4 months. The most significant improvement occurred on tests that measured attention, retention, auditory and visual comprehension, word finding, organization (sequencing and visual closure); identification of relevant and most salient features, and abstract thinking. At the completion of treatment, patients showed continued difficulty with the identification of relevant and most salient features, immediate, short term, and recent recall of information, sequencing, word finding, and problem solving. Regarding specific subtests, closed head trauma patients showed significantly improved posttreatment scores relating to description of item differences. Initially, the patients used a functional rather than a descriptive strategy, which resulted in personalized responses (e.g., when given "How are wool and silk different?," the response was, "My scarf is made of silk, my coat is made of wool"). Initially and at discharge, head injured patients had the greatest difficulty with the description of item differences and less difficulty with the description of item similarities.

When asked to provide the opposite of specified words, head injured patients tended to give synonyms rather than antonyms (e.g, "give" in response to "lend") or to add "not to" before the stimulus (e.g., "not to lend" in response to "lend"). At discharge, the patients made significant improvement in the provision of antonyms. With regard to a free recall task, closed head trauma patients utilized more strategies on posttesting, such as phonemic strategies (e.g., tin, ton, ten) and semantic strategies (e.g., snow, ski, sled). Posttesting also revealed that the patients were better able to identify verbal absurdities. Initially, when asked to tell what is absurd about this situation, "A little child was drowning in the middle of the lake. His mother shouted to her friends. 'Don't stand there doing nothing, bring me my rubbers that I may rescue my child,'" the patient's responses indicated that the point was missed – e.g., "rubbers are too short for deep water." Final posttest scores revealed an improvement in salient feature identification; for example, "Don't go out with rubbers, just jump in there as fast as you can." Finally, the most significant changes in tests scores occurred during the first month of treatment.

Research that addressed rehabilitation techniques for cognitive problems typically experienced by closed head injured patients will now be reviewed.

Perception

Visual perception requires the following abilities: eye-motor coordination, figure-ground perception, form recognition (color, shape, size), identification of position in space, and spatial relationships. Different sensory inputs can have the same stored form – that is, visually and auditorially presented words might eventually reach the same stored representation, for we make note of the psychological distinction in meaning based on this type of stimulus difference. Piaget suggests the following with regard to perceptual processes: (1) awareness within a perceptual domain (visual, auditory, tactile, or kinesthetic) exceeds awareness between domains; (2) developmentally, a topological space (awareness of a point in space or figure-ground relationships and part-whole relationships) is preceived first, followed by projective space (relationships of two or more objects), and finally euclidean space (awareness of the orientation of another as separate from that of the perceiver).

Clark (1973a and b) suggested that there are three perceptual planes when humans are in a canonical position: (1) ground level, in which the ground serves as a reference plane and upward is regarded as a positive perception; (2) the vertical, left-right plane, in which through the body serves as a reference plane and forward is considered to be a positive perception; and (3) the vertical, front-back plane, in which the front of the body serves as a reference plane and left and right are considered to be positive perceptions. The use of unmarked or positive terms occurs prior to the development of corresponding marked or negative terms. Clark believed this could be explained on a perceptual basis in such a way that positive terms are more visible. A human organism's perceptual apparatus possesses certain asymmetries in terms of the perceptual fields available. A human being standing upright has symmetrical left-right vision but asymmetrical front-back perceptual fields. The things in front are visible; the things behind are not. An individual also has an up-down asymmetry such that things on or above the earth's surface are visible, but those below normally are not. Clark suggested that perception progresses from the differentiation of simple contours to differentiated features to structure relations of patterns to unique patterns, such as the perception of individual faces.

Shaw and Cutting (1980) refer to five types of invariant-perceptual tasks: (1) spatial structure versus space, which requires the establishment of adjacency relations among co-occurring parts; (2) temporal order versus time, in which successive ordering of adjacent structures occurs; (3) events versus objects, in which events are suggested to change adjacency structures (spatiality) over successive orderings (temporality), whereas permanent objects have nonchanging adjacency structures and only relative permanence; (4) structure of events such that structural variance includes the distinguishing of one object or a class of objects from other objects; structural invariance includes those items that do not distinguish objects; (5) perception of composite events in which perception of simple events proceeds to the perception of complex events up through the operations of nesting, coordinating, and concatenating. During nesting, subordinate styles of change with relatively short temporal periods are superimposed on styles of change with relatively longer periods. For example, plays are nested events inside games, games are nested events within seasons, and so forth. Coordinating events refer to the coordination of two or more relatively independent events such as two hands in double-handed signs. Concatenative events refer to complex events that string together events so that periods follow successively. For example, an undershirt goes on before the shirt and the shirt before the tie.

Discrimination

Wetzel and Squire (1982) indicated that discriminations are differentiations between an individual and a world of experience. Cognitive distancing, that is, freeing an individual from direct experience to rely more on representations of experience, is based on a continuum that progresses from the discrimination of concrete to abstract items (e.g., objects to pictures to words.)

In piagetian theory, the reversibility operation or the ability to discriminate negation or reversal of an operation is thought to be critical to the development of quantitative thinking in all logical thought. The first step in the development of universal discrimination is the displacement of an object, which is then returned to its original place, thus negating the action. Reversibility is a critical operation necessary for the ability to deal with conservation, seriation, and classification – for example, if the concept of reversibility is lacking, it is understood that A is larger than B but at the same time B is not understood to be less than A.

Clark (1973b) referred to one-dimensional, two-dimensional, and three-dimensional types of discriminations. Far versus near and long versus short are considered to be two of the most elementary or one-dimensional types of discriminations. The extent of any one dimensional object, like a line, is called its length, and we speak of the distance from one point to the other. The difference between length and distance is that length is extensional, specifying the extent of the object, such as long or short; distance, on the other hand, is positional, specifying the position of one point with respect to another, such as far or near. Clark suggested that prepositions can be defined in terms of making reference to egocentric or nonegocentric space. Egocentric discriminations are acquired first; ego, or the person himself, is taken as a primary point of reference.

Wide versus narrow discriminations presuppose objects with two or more dimensions: discrimination of a secondary edge extending

Table 6-1. A Summary of Some Properties of English Spatial Adjectives

Adjective Pair	Extent or Position	No. of Dimensions	Unmarked point of reference	Dimension
long-short	+ extent	1	ego	length
far-near	+ position	1	ego	distance
tall-short	+ extent	3	ground level	tallness
high-low	+ position	3	ground level	height
deep-shallow	+ extent	3	any surface	depth
deep	+ position	3	any surface	depth
wide-narrow	+ extent	2	a secondary edge	width
wide	+ position	2	a secondary edge	width
broad-narrow	+ extent	2	a secondary edge	breadth
thick-thin	+ extent	3	a tertiary edge	thickness

From Clark, H.H., "Space, time, semantics, and the child". In T. Moore (Ed.), *Cognitive Development and Acquisition of Language.* New York, Academic Press, 1973, p. 40. Reprinted with permission.

beyond a reference edge (wide) or less than the reference edge (narrow). Tall versus short and high versus low are more complex in that they presuppose three-dimensional objects on a vertical plane. Tallness can refer to vertical length and height can refer to vertical distance. Both tallness and height are measured from ground level up, although the base of the objects specifies what is to be taken as ground level (i.e., "The flag pole on top of that building is very tall."). Additional adjectives with varying numbers of dimensions, and therefore, varying complexity are presented in Table 6-1.

Clark (1973b) referred to more difficult discriminations required with adjectives and prepositions that presuppose two kinds of verticality: geological and intrinsic. Certain objects have intrinsic tops

Table 6-2. Illustrative Rules of Application for
in, into, **and** *out of*

Preposition	Rules of application
A in B	1. B denotes a three-dimensional enclosed space.
A into B	1. B denotes a three-dimensional enclosed space. 2. A is moving in one direction. 3. The direction is positive.
A out of B	1. B denotes a three-dimensional enclosed space. 2. A is moving in one direction. 3. The direction is positive. 4. Rule (3) is not the case.

From Clark, H.H. "Space, time, semantics, and the child." In T. Moore (Ed.), *Cognitive Development and Acquisition of Language.* New York, Academic Press, 1973, p. 55. Reprinted with permission.

and bottoms as well as fronts and backs. Even if a bottle is turned on its side we would be able to speak of a fly on top of the bottle and mean on the side with the opening. In this case, tops and bottoms are relative to the canonical or upright position. The distinction between the gravitational top and the intrinsic top often leads to ambiguities. The following example provides an illustration: If a person is lying on the beach and another person says there is a fly three inches above your knee, this could mean that there is a fly flying three inches vertically from the knee, or there is a fly on the leg three inches headward from the knee. Clark (1973b) also proposed a complexity hypothesis, which implies that, given two terms A and B, in which B requires all the rules of the application of A plus one or more in addition, A will normally be acquired before B. An example of the complexity hypothesis can be seen in the relationships between *in, into,* and *out of,* as well as *at, on,* and *in.* For example, *in* presupposes that the object denotes an enclosed three-dimensional space. *Into* presupposes this but also implies that the subject of the proposition is moving in one direction, which is positive. *Out of* presupposes all of the above but has an implicit negative, suggesting that the motion of the object is not positive. The discriminations required by the complexity hypothesis are illustrated in Table 6-2.

Organization

Categorization is one type of organizational activity. Rosch (1973) suggested that items are categorized based on perceptual features, such as color and form (e.g., red balloon and a red ball); nonperceptual semantic features that have internal structures affect the way they are processed, such as modes of transportation (e.g., a motorcycle and a truck). Therefore, both physiological and psychological factors are involved in categorization. The psychological reality of internal structure implies that the abstract formal definition of the category or the critical attributes that define it as a good or less good category member may be different attributes that are defined in a more abstract way. The attributes may differ in the extent to which they represent a core meaning of the category. For example, the distinction between wild and domestic is irrelevant to the formal definition of bird; however, wild birds are judged more central to the bird category than are domestic ones. Quite often, the most common members of a category become the best examples of the category. Another explanation is that cultures come to define as best examples of a category those members that are maximally different from other categories to be maximally discriminable. Salient members of one category were not also in another category. Rosch further suggested that categories whose central members are in their own right easier to learn will be learned more quickly than categories whose central members are more difficult to learn.

At the simplest level, categorization can be initiated by the matching and sorting of geometric objects and pictures through the use of games. Associations in the same category as the stimuli are paradigmatic associations. Associations that cross categories are nonparadigmatic. Annett (1959) used a standard card-sorting task to investigate free classification. The subjects were required to state verbally the reason for each group formed. Five types of verbalizations were differentiated: (1) no explanation; (2) enumeration (e.g., dog, cat, horse); (3) contiguity (e.g., apple, tree); (4) similarity (e.g., hat, cap); and (5) class names (e.g., animals). Annett found that categorization abilities varied as a function of age. The five and six year olds did not sort on the basis of common characteristics and frequently did not explain responses. "No explanation" responses decreased sharply with an increase in age. Before age seven, verbal enumerations of items predominated; after that age they decreased. The seven and eight year olds grouped items into parts–for example; screw and screwdriver.

The use of contiguity criteria peaked at age eight and then declined. By age nine, and through early adulthood, items were grouped into categories or classes based on similar criteria. In addition to these developmental changes, an increase in the number of items within each category and a decrease in number of categories formed was observed with an increase in age. Annett suggested that the development of concept formation progresses from concrete to abstract level of classification. At the more concrete levels, spatial and temporal cues as well as perceptual and functional characteristics were the basis for such groups. At the more abstract level, items were grouped on the basis of less observable characteristics, frequently involving symbols.

Clark (1973b) suggested that time is not expressed just occasionally with a spatial simile, but rather is based totally on a semantic spatial metaphor, suggesting that space and time expressions have a common cognitive system. Time and space concepts require organizational skills, including categorization and sequencing. Since time is a spatial metaphor, the use of a term to denote time must be preceded by the acquisition of a comparable term to denote space. Thus, spatial expressions should appear before time expressions—for example, comprehension of a "long stick" occurs before comprehension of psychological dimensions such as "a long time." The time concept first develops between the ages of one and a half to four years. At this early age, thought is egocentric as the child lives in the present, and it is irreversible because each movement succeeds another. The development of the concept of time requires comprehension of the nature of the coordination of motions at different velocities, including external objects as they relate to physical time and the person himself as he relates to psychological time.

Problem Solving

Regarding conservation, Halford (1980) suggested that subjects are required to interpret an ambiguous act which, when taken by itself, might be thought of as increasing quantity. Children make the transition to conservation when they widened the data base that they used in making judgments about quantities. Transformation such as pouring into a taller and narrower vessel, may seem in the short term to increase the quantity but in the long term it does not. Therefore, the child must consider long-term rather than short-term consequences of the transformation.

As a therapy activity, Notelting (1975) showed children two large pitchers, A and B, and told the children he was going to dump several tumblers of orange juice and several tumblers of water into each pitcher. The children were to predict which pitcher would taste more strongly of orange juice. The normal children used the following strategies to solve this task: (1) Children ages three to four and a half were able to focus on one global feature: the presence or absence of juice and succeeded only when one side received juice; (2) children ages four and a half to six noticed not only the presence or absence of juice on each side but also the quantity of juice. They began to use counting to compare the amount of juice on each side and picked the side with the greater number of juice tumblers, saying that side would taste more strongly of juice; (3) children ages seven and eight noticed the number of water tumblers on each side as well as the number of juice containers and counted the number of water and juice containers; they picked the side having the excessive juice over water, but if both sides had excess juice over water they simply guessed; and (4) children nine years of age succeeded in any item in which simple ratios were involved. The only limitation in this stage was that there are progressively increasing demands on working memory as the steps necessary to solve the problem have to be held in working memory.

Becker, Bender, and Morrison (1978) used three piagetian conservation of space tasks to evaluate the abilities of children with or without learning disabilities to revisualize special boundaries. A total of 169 children were studied, including 125 children with learning disabilities in grades 1 through 5. The children were presented with two drawings of the same objects. On two of the tasks, one of the objects was in an upright position and the other was rotated to 45 degrees or 90 degrees. On the third task only one tilted object was presented. On the upright object a mark indicating a liquid line was drawn. The child's task was to relocate the line on the rotated object. On another task, the child was presented with a ball on which a chain was hanging down from the top. The child was to draw the ball and chain when the box was tilted 45 degrees. On the final task, a jar tilted 90 degrees was placed under a faucet and imaginary water was running into it. The child was to draw the line indicating the orientation of the imagined line when the jar was filled. Children with and without learning disabilities performed similarly and all three tasks were equally easy. A significant effect was obtained for grade level. Younger children did not correctly revisualize as many of the spatial relocations as did older children.

Another conservation task involves use of two stimuli, which begin as equal. One of the stimuli is transformed in pattern, and the individual must decide if the stimuli should continue to be judged equal. For example, two equal balls of clay are presented. One is squashed and one is rolled into a cigar. Alternatively, liquid in a tall thin container is poured into a short thick container. The ability to deal with these problems occurs in Piaget's concrete and formal operational stage, which is suggested to occur between ages seven and eleven. During this time the child is thought to have some grasp of logical reasoning.

With regard to antonyms and synonyms, Muma (1978) found that children picked objects that were the same, when asked to choose one that was the same and when asked to choose one that was different. It was suggested that the ability to identify synonyms develops before the ability to identify antonyms. Adamovich and Henderson (1982, 1983) found that closed head injured patients also showed this pattern of task difficulty. However, Adamovich and Brooks (1981) found that the reverse was true with subjects who had sustained right hemisphere damage secondary to cerebrovascular accidents. These subjects experienced more success providing antonyms than synonyms.

Piaget (1966) distinguished two types of logic. Formal logic refers to the recognition of signs of truth conditions. Operational logic is necessary to disengage the logical structure of psychological or mental facts. The development of higher level reasoning can be closely related to the child's level of tolerance for unclosed operations.

Simple analogies require the ability to represent internally a single relationship, which is compared with each of two situations (i.e., man is to boy as dog is to puppy requires recognition of the relationship of parent). This is generally understood by a normal child age three to four. Subjects are unable to realize analogies for several reasons: (1) an inability to apply story analogies; (2) an inability to locate analogies in memory; and (3) failure to spontaneously accept the relevance of the analogies to target problems even though potentially useful analogies are retrieved. Bower (1978) suggested that the mapping process involved in analogies may play a role in a variety of cognitive skills. Using analogy involves mapping representations of two or more instances into one another. A further suggestion is that the mapping process for analogies involves three distinct but interrelated activities: (1) comparing one instance to another; (2) deriving a schema for a class of instances; and (3) comparing one instance to a general schema. A better understanding of how analogies are retrieved and noticed is essential to teach the use of analogies as strategies for problem solving (Bower, 1978). Kirby and Biggs (1980) suggested that children pass through a sequence of substances in each major piagetian stage in which their strategies or roles for approaching a problem for that stage become increasingly complex. A condition necessary for strategy restructuring is the exposure to information relevant to a specific question. A second necessary condition for improved problem solving is an increase in working memory space for coordinating the information. Other reasons for the improved use of strategies are the development of motivation and improved ability to use feedback (Gholson and McConville, 1974; Parrill-Burnstein, 1978).

Craik and Lockhart (1972) suggested that problem solving is composed of three basic processes: (1) translation of the problem into a model; (2) operation on the model to make necessary deductions; and (3) retranslation back to the problem situation. Internal representation of the problem can take a variety of forms, depending on the type of problem, past experience, the cognitive style, and the problem solver.

Ben-Yishay (1980) reported that training normal reasoning required the following steps: (1) a motive of the problem is recognized; (2) the problem is formulated within a context; (3) the conditions of the problem are analyzed; (4) a strategy or approach is formulated; (5) the operations, tactics, or plans are chosen; (6) the plan of action is executed or solved; and (7) the solution to the problem is rechecked.

When teaching problem-solving skills or didactic considerations, Ben-Yishay (1980) indicated that the following steps should occur: (1) the patient should be taught to ask the right questions to get at central features of the problems; (2) the task should be broken down to meaningful units; and (3) a system of gradual cueing should be established.

Bruner (1973) identified two types of problem-solving strategies. The first and most efficient was the focusing of holistic strategy. This strategy was observed when a child selects and evaluates an initial hypothesis on the basis of all the information encountered. The second and less efficient strategy was a scanning strategy, in which problem solvers processed instances either successively or in parts, so that not all the information encountered was processed at one time.

Several investigators have designed tasks to treat problem-solving deficits with children. A task analysis approach was incorporated into the classic remedial procedures of Johnson and

Mykelbust (1967). Finch and Spirito (1980) designed a successful procedure, which they referred to as Cognitive Behavior Modification Tasks. Their approach stressed a hierarchical and sequential relationship between the steps necessary to solve the problem. Task analysis was employed when teaching a specific skill or strategy. When a specific skill was taught, such as learning to remember a group of objects, the child was exposed to a sequence of steps necessary to acquire that skill. In teaching a strategy, several tasks that were similar with regard to stimuli, responses, and format were analyzed into similar sequences and taught.

Meichenbaum (1980) used self-instructional techniques with children with many different types of clinical problems. For example, he first used his approach successfully in training hyperactive or impulsive children to stop, look, and think about all alternative courses of action rather than pouncing on the first available answer. The children were first taught the plan by watching a model demonstrate the behavior, which was described step by step by the clinician. Then the children performed the behavior while describing the steps aloud. Next, the behavior was performed while the steps were subvocalized. Finally, the children were to think of the instructions while performing the behavior. The most effective instructions were those specific to the critical features of the task and those which described exactly what was to be done to succeed. Parrill-Burnstein (1981) trained groups of children to solve problems using one of four conditions. Children in group one enumerated verbally four cues or salient features of the problem. Children in group two were given both verbal and visual representations of the salient features of the problem. In addition to strategies taught to group two, children in group three were taught to complete a sequence of problem solving steps. Children in group four were taught all the strategies and were also given information about how to respond appropriately to feedback. They were taught to eliminate or remove an incorrect hypothesis and retest or leave a confirmed hypothesis. The problem solving skills of children in the fourth group improved significantly more than children in the other groups as judged by a post test.

Chapter 7

Theoretical Considerations: Neurophysiological Theories

GENERAL PRINCIPLES

The ability to attend is necessary for all levels of information analysis and recall. Attention is a process of stimulus selection (Ross, 1976) or selective perception (Pick, Frankel and Hess, 1975). Attention is the capacity to apprehend and manipulate multiple aspects of a stimulus situation at any moment in time. When attending, an individual must focus on salient aspects of a given stimulus and, at the same time, on irrelevant, extraneous stimuli (Gazzaniga and Sperry, (1967). In addition, more than one channel of attention is available at any given time, which requires individuals to switch their attention from one message or situation to another (Norman, 1968).

Theories of Attention

Theories of attention include the following: (1) theory of specificity (Gibson, 1969; Pick et al., 1975); (2) gestalt perceptual theory of learning (Asch, 1961; Kohler, 1941); and (3) information processing theory (Broadbent, 1958; Craik and Lockhart, 1972; Dykman, Ackerman, and Clements, 1971; Neisser, 1976). The theory of specificity as proposed by Pick and co-workers (1975) describes attention as a process of selection. The selection process is thought to be an ongoing process rather than an isolated construct that occurs as part of the cognitive activities of perception, memory, and thought. Gibson (1969) suggested that perception becomes more specific or differentiated and precise during information processing. The receiver does not learn to process previously unavailable stimuli but instead becomes better at extracting additional information that was not picked up by the perceiver initially, even though it was available in the environment. Gibson suggested that this occurred due to (1) the recognition of critical properties that differentiate stimuli; (2) filtration of irrelevant stimuli; and (3) integration of perceived information.

The gestalt perceptual theory of learning as described by Kohler (1941) emphasized the process of differentiation and perceptual development. Attention is viewed as an ongoing part of perception. Perceptual learning is the result of the reorganization or dynamic redistribution of neurological activity. Associations are the aftereffects of perception, which may persist as memory traces to be activated later. These associations are based on perceptual relationships, which are a function of the total configuration of the situation or the gestalt. This theory was predominant in the 1950s and early 1960s.

During the late 1960s and early 1970s, the study of attention shifted to evaluation of physiological changes and information processing (Dykman et al., 1971). Dykman and associates suggested that learning disabilities resulted from organically based deficits resulting in decreased attention. These deficits were attributed to neurological immaturity and were manifested as a developmental lag. Specific deficits and abilities to inhibit responding to irrelevant stimuli were noted. Deficits in attention occurred at the levels of alertness, stimulus attention, stimulus selection, and vigilance. These problems were symptoms of a more generalized deficit, sustaining attention, which was accompanied by a decrease in physiological activity that changed as a function of maturation and experience.

In general, the information processing theorists concluded that processing of global characteristics occurs first as a child develops, followed by the processing of more specific attributes. This can be referred to as selective attention, or selective perception, reflecting the interrelationships of attention and perception. The most prevalent view with respect to the role of the perceiver is that he or she perceives as an active participant rather than a passive observer. An adjustable threshold of attention presensitizes the organism to sensory information of high relevance or pertinence in the selective filter model suggested by Broadbent (1958). The question of limited capacity has not yet been resolved, although at present it receives some support (Adamovich, 1981; McNeil, 1981).

Craik and Lockhart (1972) suggested that what is retained by adults is a function of the level or depth of processing required by the orienting task. These authors hypothesized that the stimulus is first encoded and analyzed at a perceptual level. The memory trace is a byproduct of this perceptual analysis. The persistence of the trace is determined by the depth or level at which it is processed.

Depth of processing refers to how elaborate or deep the analysis of the item is. The levels of analysis imply a hierarchy of stages through which incoming information can progress in order to be remembered. These stages may involve sensory, perceptual, and cognitive analyses. Based on the theory that the mind is a complex of abilities, the powers of observation, attention, memory, thinking, and so on, would all be improved if an improvement in one specific ability occurred. Craik and Lockhart suggested that mental abilities function independently of the material with which they operate, and the development of one ability entails the development of others. Ben-Yishay (1978) suggested that individuals must have maximum attention, concentration, and persistence to participate in verbal logical reasoning. For example, retention is affected by the attention devoted to the stimulus with respect to the analysis of structures and the processing time available. An individual ability or inability to direct attention is an essential determinant of the success or failure of any practical operation. As attention improves or expands, individuals become capable of reconstructing their perception and, therefore, become free from the auditory or visual field. Behavior is regulated not solely by the salience of individual elements but also by the individual's evaluation of the relative importance of these elements in a given situation. Changes in the immediate situation can be viewed based on past activities and on anticipation of the future (Craik and Lockhart, 1972).

Analysis of Attention

Factors to be considered during analyses of attention include arousal, attentiveness, and vigilance. Arousal is associated with physiological dimension – that is, a continuum in which sleep is at one extreme and wakefulness is at the other. Attentiveness refers to the readiness of the organism to perceive incoming stimulation. Vigilance refers to the ability to maintain attentiveness (Parrill-Burnstein, 1981). Arousal is basic to information processing. However, inappropriate, excessive arousal also interferes with information processing as it tends to lessen the space available in short-term memory. Biofeedback techniques might be useful to teach individuals to control their own levels of arousal.

Disruption of Attention

Attentional disruptions can be caused by disinhibition, hyperactivity, and distractibility. Disinhibition is distraction by inner factors. Distractibility is attention to irrelevant factors within the environment, and hyperactivity is due to excessive motor performance. Slowing of attentional processes leads to slow orientation to a new mental set, an inability to shift sets, difficulty producing ideas spontaneously in spite of the fact responses are made to externally structured commands, and a slowing in serial tasks that require rapid reorientation from one step to another.

Ross (1976) suggested the major bases for problems described as learning disabilities are abnormal developments of attentional processes that depend on appropriate or optimal cortical arousal. According to Doyle, Anderson and Holcomb (1976), children with learning disabilities tend to pay more attention to extraneous visual stimuli than do children without learning disabilities. These children also showed evidence of disinhibition, poor stimulus selection, and problems sustaining attention. According to Anderson (1973), the children made more false alarms and detected fewer correct stimuli during vigilance task performance.

The possibility of disruption of arousal systems and attentional abilities must be considered with head injured subjects. Most scales of recovery usually refer to a sequence of behavioral changes following closed head trauma from onset of coma through various levels of confusional states and on to relative recover stages. Behavioral changes described include the following: (1) level of arousal; (2) degree of confusion; (3) presence of posttraumatic amnesia; (4) degree of agitation and outbursts; and (5) functional ability to participate in activities of daily living. In a recent review, Alexander (1982) identified a seven-stage behavioral hierarchy following closed head trauma: (1) coma; (2) unresponsive vigilance; (3) mute responsiveness; (4) confusional state; (5) independent in daily self-care with adequate social interaction; (6) independent intellectual function; and (7) complete social recovery. Patients recover or move from one stage to the next at varying rates, and recovery can be arrested at any stage. The evolution of recovery through this continuum will be referred to as the general recovery of mental control functions. Specific areas that are included under mental control are attention, orientation, and certain types of memory deficits.

Mental Control Function

"Mental control function" is thought to represent the ability to manipulate the focus of attention in three basic ways: (1) initiating and sustaining attention; (2) shifting the focus of attention when appropriate; and (3) inhibiting the inappropriate shifting of the focus of attention. A disorder in the ability to *initiate* attention characterizes the comatose patient. An inability to *sustain* attention is usually referred to as a confusional state. Confusion has been described as a global disorder of attention. A standard test of the ability to sustain attention is the familiar digit span. The inability to *appropriately* shift the focus of attention can be seen as perseveration. The patient's responses may become linked to an internal or external stimulus. The inability to *appropriately inhibit the shifting* of the focus of attention is usually manifested as disinhibition, distractibility, or impulsivity. At times, the target of an inappropriate shift may not be obvious and may become evident only as an odd intrusion.

Geschwind (1982) recently discussed the importance of considering attentional disorders. He described five features of attentional systems that should be considered in any assessment: selectivity, coherence, universality, distractibility, and sensitivity to specific circumstances. The most important point is that a disorder of attention should not be considered a simple inability to maintain vigilance.

In higher stages of recovery, the disorder of mental control may persist as a difficulty in concentration and may be seen even following minor head injury. The components of the mental control function are fragile and can be exposed when the patient is confronted with complex tasks, competing stimuli, or tasks that depend on speed of performance. Therefore, even when the patient may no longer be confused in the traditional sense (i.e., when his or her digit span is normal), the disorder of mental control can be exposed by asking the patient to perform in a distractible environment or to handle more complex problems, which require the manipulation of several pieces of information. The inability to handle multiple, nonlinear pieces of information is a cardinal feature of many of the cognitive deficits of closed head trauma subjects. Problem solving, for example, requires the patient to handle multiple bits of information and to shift the focus of attention between them in an appropriate manner. Therefore, difficulty in mental control will result in a breakdown in problem-solving abilities. Not uncommonly, the patient may commit an error in the early stages of learning a sequence of activities and then commit an identical error in all future attempts at that sequence (a form of perseveration).

Emotional responses, such as agitation, impulsiveness, and disinhibition, that are seen in the closed head injured patient can parallel disorders of mental control. Agitation and outbursts in the early stages of recovery can be viewed as impulsive responses to internal or external stimuli. Stimuli that may provoke a minimal response of annoyance in a normal person may result in an impulsive, uninhibited response by a patient with a disorder of mental control, which usually begins with frustration, anger, and then agitation. The clinician should be careful to identify situations that increase agitation and attempt to avoid them. Patients with diffuse brain injuries will often become agitated as a consequence of a disorder in mental control. This agitation would be regarded as a somewhat typical stage in the recovery process.

It appears that most scales of recovery can be viewed as scales of mental control functions. For example, independence in daily self-care with adequate social interaction will result when the patient acquires sufficient mental control to perform such tasks and is able to inhibit inappropriate, impulsive outbursts. Independent intellectual function implies further evolution along the continuum, with a resolution of the impairments in communication, memory, organization of information, and visuoperceptual skills that can be secondary to the primary impairment in mental control. Other features contribute to functional recovery, such as psychosocial factors, sensorimotor limitations, and deficits attributable to other discrete focal lesions (aphasias, true amnesias, and so forth). Nevertheless, delineation of the progression along a continuum of mental control will allow the clinician to determine the potential contribution of these other factors.

It could be predicted that the tests that emphasize over-learned material and do not place a premium on mental control tasks and problem-solving abilities should plateau within a few months. For instance, verbal IQ subtests of the Wechsler Adult Intelligence Scale (WAIS) do not stress problem-solving skills. Performance subtests of the WAIS, on the other hand, do stress the ability to solve problems, often with time restrictions. Several long-term studies have demonstrated that recovery of verbal IQ plateaus by six months but that performance IQ scores may not reach a plateau until 12 months or later (Smith, 1974). Furthermore, if the length of posttraumatic amnesia is taken as a measure of severity of injury, it should be possible to predict a correlation between severity of injury and recovery on the performance IQ and other tests of decision making or reaction time. Indeed, the plateau of verbal IQ scores correlates poorly with the severity of injury, whereas the plateau of performance IQ scores correlates more closely, and tests of information processing and decision making correlate even more closely (Smith, 1974).

Mandelberg (1976) examined the recovery of verbal Intelligence

Quotients (VIQ) and performance Intelligence Quotients (PIQ) of the WAIS in patients with severe nonpenetrating head injuries. He noted that the rate of recovery appeared to correlate with the severity of the posttraumatic confusional state (as measured by the duration of the posttraumatic amnesia). In particular, the VIQ reached a relative plateau within three to six months. The VIQ relies heavily on previously learned material, and little emphasis is placed on problem-solving ability. Interestingly, this recovery curve is quite comparable to the pattern of recovery seen in discrete focal lesions, in which recovery reaches a relative plateau in about three to six months. The PIQ, on the other hand, requires a higher degree of problem solving, and hence a greater degree of set shifting and manipulation of the focus of attention. Obviously, the PIQ will be more sensitive than the VIQ to a disorder of mental control function. As expected, the PIQ did not reach its relative plateau for 6 to 12 months. The PIQ also tended to be consistently lower than the VIQ.

The impact of the disorder of mental control can be seen in the work of Gronwall (1977). The Paced Auditory Serial Addition Test (PASAT), was used to study patients suffering minor closed head injuries. In the PASAT, a tape recorded series of digits is presented and the patient is asked to add the numbers serially. For instance, if the first three numbers are 3, 5, 4, the patient would wait until after the second digit is presented and say "8." After the third digit, the patient would say "12." The speed of the presentation can be varied by varying the interstimulus interval. Gronwall has shown that improvement on the PASAT parallels the course of recovery. On examining the PASAT it becomes apparent that the abilities to sustain attention, to shift from stimulus to stimulus, and to inhibit distractions or inappropriate shifting are all critical. Speed also plays an additional role in performance. The disorder of divided attention as measured by the PASAT seems to represent the disorder of mental control.

RESEARCH: SPECIFIC THERAPY IMPLICATIONS

Once a response is elicited, the goal of treatment should be to increase the frequency of occurrence, duration, and variety of the response. Clinicians should consider the duration of attention and should not go much beyond that in treatment sessions even if it means that therapy sessions have to be brief and frequent throughout the day.

Keogh and Margolis (1976) studied the ability to sustain attention within an educational context. These researchers analyzed three components of attention: (1) coming to attention; (2) making decisions; and (3) sustaining attention. Coming to attention involved two aspects: overcoming extraneous and possibly disruptive motor activity and the selection and organization of the salient, relevant aspects of the task. Keogh (1971) suggested that hyperactive children demonstrated deficits at this level of attention. Next, analyses of decision making considered the tempo or speed of the response. Analyses of attention maintenance considered the ability to sustain attention. These investigators found that learning disabled children had problems with all three of these attentional components.

Torgensen (1979) found that directing a child's attention to the stimuli to be remembered increased the child's ability to recall the information. Norman (1968) suggested that knowledge of the message can be facilitated by aiding the perceptual process prior to presentation of the signal by calling attention to various features to which the person might not be attending. Inputs that are not highly pertinent may not be recognized until their pertinence level has been raised. Raising the levels of pertinence for certain items was found to be equivalent to lowering the threshold for the sensory inputs corresponding to these items. It was suggested that this should be a focus of treatment.

Parrill-Burnstein (1981) found that preschool children tend to attend to the most salient characteristics of the stimulus, to position cues, and to random items. Between ages five and seven, children were able to scan a visual array more systematically. At approximately age six, children were able to direct attention toward a recognized goal, and children of ages 10 and 14 were able to recall more central or task-relevant information. Offenbach (1974) recommended a selective attention procedure in which subjects were required to focus attention, through overt selection, on a specific hypothesis. His suggested procedure proved effective in increasing selective attention to hypotheses and in facilitating certain problem solving behaviors. Cruickshank (1966) suggested that the treatment of attentional deficits experienced by learning disabled children should provide for the following: (1) physical organization of the classroom, which is to avoid overstimulation and to provide for multisensory processing; and (2) provision of concrete material due to the possibilities of perceptual dysfunction.

Chapter 8

Assessment of Cognitive Abilities

Suggested methods that are currently under test to diagnose and assess cognitive processing are presented in this chapter. Specific functions to be tested have been arranged in a hierarchical fashion beginning with low level skills. This evaluation includes tasks to assess arousal or alerting, perception or low level selective attention, discrimination, orientation, organization, recall, and high level thought processes, including convergent thinking, deductive reasoning, inductive reasoning, divergent thinking, and multiprocess reasoning. It was believed that this arrangement would facilitate treatment planning, as breakdown in performance would indicate an appropriate place to initiate therapy. Specific treatment techniques for each stage in the proposed hierarchy are presented in Chapter 9.

AROUSAL AND ALERTING

Complete the following tasks designed to test the ability to respond at a reflexive level. Note presence or absence and types of responses elicited. (Total possible points: 3.)

1. Ring a bell near the patient.
2. Place a rubber spoon on the patient's lips in an attempt to elicit a chewing, sucking and/or a biting reflex.
3. Stroke the side of patient's face, beginning at the corner of the mouth and going across the cheek in an attempt to elicit a rooting reflex.

PERCEPTUAL OR LOW LEVEL SELECTIVE ATTENTION

Tasks at this level are designed to test the integration and interpretation of information received at the sense organs based on an internal or stored representation of the stimulus. Cognitive processing begins at this level.

Tracking

1. Visual: Instruct the patient to watch a light. Note patient's ability to follow the light to the right, left, up, and down. (Total possible points: 4.)

2. Auditory: Instruct the patient to close his or her eyes and listen for a bell. Once bell has been rung, the patient is to look toward the bell. Note the patient's ability to follow sound to the right, left, front, back and various locations in the room. (Total possible points: 5.)

Sound Recognition

Ask the patient to raise his or her hand when a horn is sounded in a tape recording of the following randomized sounds: buzz, telephone, and click. The horn sound should be presented five times during the recording. (Total possible points: 5.)

Shape Recognition

Ask the patient to copy a vertical line, circle, square, and the letter B. Record number of correct responses. (Total possible points: 4.)

Word Recognition

Instruct the patient to raise his or her hand every time he or she hears the word *blue* in a tape recording of the following paragraph. Record the number of correct responses. (Total possible points: 10.)

Last night I was feeling *blue* when I came home from work driving my *blue* car. I glanced into the *blue* sky and saw some rain clouds. My brother, nicknamed "Big *Blue*," was in the house wearing a *blue* shirt and *blue* pants. He told me he was taking me to dinner at the *Blue* Lagoon. I put on a *blue* outfit and we drove off. As I glanced across the street with my big *blue* eyes, I notice three identical *blue blouses hanging on the line.*

Word Recognition in Noise

Instruct the patient to raise his or her hand every time he or she hears the word *baseball* in a tape recording of the following paragraph. The recording should be made with typical cafeteria noise in the background. Record the number of correct responses. (Total possible points: 10.)

Baseball is the national sport of the United States. The game of *baseball* includes nine players on each side. There are two *baseball* leagues; these are the National and the American *baseball* teams, including the Cleveland Indians, the Boston Red Sox, and the Philadelphia Phillies *baseball* teams. The game of *baseball* was first played in New England in the 1800s. Equipment used in a *baseball* game includes a bat, ball, gloves, and bases. *Baseball* fans in the bleachers are usually most boisterous. Beer and hot dogs are popular things to eat and drink while watching a *baseball* game.

DISCRIMINATION

The purpose of this subtest is to test the ability to differentiate two or more stimuli.

Visual

Color, shape, and size. Use two red circles, two yellow circles, two blue circles, two red triangles, two red squares, three large yellow squares, and three small yellow squares cut out of colored paper.

Color. Place six circles on a table in front. Place two red, two yellow, and two blue circles on a table in front of the patient. Ask the patient to point to the blue forms. Record the number of correct responses. (Total possible points: 2.)

Shape. Place two red circles, two red triangles, and two red squares on a table in front of the patient. Ask the patient to point to the squares. Record the number of correct responses. (Total possible points: 2.)

Size. Place three large yellow squares and three small yellow squares on a table in front of the patients. Ask the patient to point to the small squares. Record the number of correct responses. (Total possible points: 3.)

Color, Shape, and Size. Place all the items on a table in front of the patient. Ask the patient to do the following: Point to a red circle, point to a yellow square, point to a large blue circle, point to a small red triangle. Record the number of correct responses. (Total possible points: 4.)

Auditory

Words. Ask the patient to identify the words named in written word strings placed on a table in front of him or her. Record the number of correct responses. (Total possible points: 3.)

1. "Point to the word house."
Given: house, horse, home, hoot, mouse.
2. "Point to the word tree."
Given: trunk, three, tree, free, tee.
3. "Point to the word walk."
Given: wake, run, wait, wall, walk.

Pictures/Objects

1. Ask the patient to verbally name the following pictures: dog, toothbrush, gate, broccoli, compass.

2. Ask the patient to write the names of the following pictured items: cup, comb, fence, telescope, funnel.

Scoring: Record the number of correct responses. (Total possible points: 5 verbal; 5 graphic.) Note the type of error responses (neologism, literal paraphasia, verbal paraphasia, other). Note the number of delayed responses (responses not initiated within 5 seconds).

Sentences — OK if have picture cards

Given a choice of two visually presented sentences, ask the patient to match the correct sentence to the stimulus picture. Record the number of correct responses. (Total possible points: 3.)

1. Picture: Woman holding dog.
   Sentences: She picked up the dog.
                 She picked at the dog.
2. Picture: Girl holding the string of a balloon that is above her shoulder.
   Sentences: The balloon is above her shoulder.
                 The balloon is beside her shoulder.
3. Picture: Boy approaching school.
   Sentences: The boy is walking toward school
                 The boy is walking away from school.

Two Step Discrimination

Instruct the patient to raise his or her hand each time he or she hears a number immediately followed by a color in the following word string, tape recorded at one word per second. Record the number of correct responses. (Total possible points: 2.)

Red, two, house, seven, yellow, three, four, green, dog, cat, blue, green, eight, rabbit.

ORIENTATION

Ask the patient the following questions. Record the number of correct responses. (Total possible points: 7.)

1. What is your name?
2. Where are you now?
3. Why are you here?
4. What day of the week is it?
5. What month is it?

6. What year is it?
7. What is today's date?

ORGANIZATION

The purpose of this subtest is to test the ability to deal with discrete actions or components that must be grouped or sequenced according to the priority of each component using a learned strategy. Three general areas are included: categorization, closure, and sequencing.

Categorization

receptive tests

1. Randomly place pictures of three colors, three vegetables, three transportation vehicles, and three animals before the patient. Ask the patient to sort the items into categories. Record the number of reasonable category placements. (Total possible points: 12.)
2. Place pictures of a bottle, jar, glass, cup, vase, chair, bed, flower, and strainer in front of the patient. Ask the patient to point to the pictures of items that hold water. Record the number of correct responses. (Total possible points: 5.)
3. Ask the patient to verbally describe the characteristics of a shoe, scissors, and a button. Score one point for each item for which the patient provides at least four correct descriptors (color, shape, size, function, and so forth). (Total possible points: 3.)
4. Ask the patient to verbally describe the likenesses and differences of the following items. Score one point for each correct likeness and one point for each correct difference. (Total possible points: 6.)
   a. spring-fall
   b. newspaper-magazine
   c. cheer-comfort

Closure

1. Show the patient the following words. Ask the patient to determine what words could be constructed if the missing letters were filled in. Score one point for each correct answer. (Total possible points: 5.)

h __ t	(hat, hit, hot, hut)
p__s__	(past, pest, post)
t__b__e	(table)
ho__id____	(holiday)
va__u____m	(vacuum)

2. Ask the patient to name the following words, which are presented one sound at a time. Record the number of correct responses. (Total possible points: 3.)

p-o-t
c-r-a-d-l-e
s-e-p-a-r-a-t-e

Sequencing

1. Sequencing shapes according to size: Ask the patient to set in order six triangles of varying sizes from the smallest to the largest triangle. Record number of triangles sequenced correctly (Total possible points: 6.)

2. Sequencing letters to form words: Ask the patient to reorder letters presented visually to form words. Record the number of correct responses. (Total possible points: 5.)

e t l	(let)
y p o c	(copy)
f a o s	(sofa)
l i d u b	(build)
t e i n v s	(invest)

3. Sequencing visually presented sentences to form a meaningful paragraph: Ask the patient to number the following sentences according to which one comes first, second, third, and so forth. Give one point for each sentence numbered correctly. (Total possible points: 5.)

_____ On August 7, 1783, he married Constance Weber.

_____ At the age of three, Wolfgang started to play the harpsicord.

_____ Wolfgang Mozart was born on January 27, 1756.

_____ Mozart was most prosperous during the years 1784-1785.

_____ He became a member of the Philharmonic Society at age 14.

4. Sequencing visually presented steps in an event: The patient is to number the following steps according to what must happen first, second, third, and so forth. Give one point for each step numbered correctly. (Total possible points: 6.)

_____ Fly to your destination.

_____ Pick up tickets at the airport.

_____ Drive to the airport.

_____ Check into a hotel.

_____ Call the travel agent to make reservations.

_____ Board the plane.

5. Verbal sequencing of steps to a task: Ask patient to give four steps necessary to make a call from a telephone booth. (Total possible points: 4.)

RECALL

Immediate, delayed (short-term), and free recall are assessed in this subtest. Notation should be made of the number of items recalled versus the number given; the type of stimuli presented (e.g., linguistic versus nonlinguistic, related versus unrelated, and so forth); the mode of stimulus presentation (e.g., visual versus aural); and apparent strategies utilized (e.g., verbal description, visual imagery, categorization, rehearsal, use of associations, temporal or spatial orientation, and primacy and recency).

Present the following words strings at the rate of one per second.

1. In the immediate, no delay condition, ask the patient to immediately repeat the words and sentences in the order given. Present the sentences at a slow, natural rate by live voice or tape recording.

2. In the delay condition, a 30 second lag should occur between the stimulus presentation and the patient's response. Record the number of words recalled overall and the number of words recalled in correct order. Make note of any patterns suggesting recall strategies—for example, last items recalled (recency effect), first items recalled (primary effect), similar word strings recalled better than dissimilar word strings, grouping or chunking of words in particular way; or verbal rehearsal.

   a. Immediate recall: Similar and dissimilar words. Total Possible points: 35 overall, 35 in correct order.
     1. tape – hat
     2. goat – lion – frog
     3. rug – song – jar – plum
     4. cow – dog – horse – lamb – rate
     5. doll – pear – bed – cup – nose – string
     6. fish – sheep – cat – bird – deer – mouse – bat

   b. Delayed recall: Similar and dissimilar words. Total possible points: 35 overall, 35 in correct order.
     1. bowl – plant
     2. gloves – socks – shirt
     3. chair – man – rock – heart
     4. hat – slacks – dress – scarf – coat
     5. man – seat – night – can – sun – knob
     6. tie – ring – boots – robe – suit – gown – shorts
     7. light – pen – stove – car – pool – tree – glass – book

   c. Delayed recall: Related sentences. Total possible points: 50 overall, 50 in correct order.
     1. George had a boat.

2. He kept it docked near home.
3. George's boat was red, black, and white.
4. He took the boat on the water today.
5. The boat sank near the shore soon after it was launched.
6. George swam to shore and called the coast guard for help.

d. Delayed recall with interference: Tell the patient: "I'm going to say three words that I want you to remember. Let's practice them. The words are *red, plant, meat*. Now what were those three words? [Patient is to repeat the words. Clinician should continue this until patient is able to repeat the three words.] Remember those words because I'll ask you again in a few minutes".

Ask the patient to answer the following questions. In questions 4 and 7, record number of words recalled. (Total possible points: 6 overall, 6 in correct order.)
1. What is the month?
2. What is the year?
3. What day of the week is it?
4. What were those three words that I asked you to remember?
5. What therapy are you having now?
6. What is the last meal you ate today?
7. What were those three words that I asked you to remember?

e. Ask the patient to listen to the following paragraph. Instruct the patient that he or she will be asked to recall the eight target words, which will be identified by the clinician during the presentation of the paragraph with the statement "remember the word." Mrs. Jones got up each morning and prepared for work (remember the word work). She first took a shower (remember the word shower). She would then prepare a small breakfast (remember the word breakfast). She then dressed, locked up and drove to the steel plant (remember the word plant). She started work at 8:00 am at the sound of the whistle (remember the word whistle). At noon each day, she would meet her friends and eat lunch (remember the word lunch). At three o'clock, the shift ended and she drove home (remember the word home). School would begin to let out at about 4:00 pm and she would greet her children (remember the word children). (Total possible points: 8.)

f. Instruct the patient to recall as many words as he or she can that begin with the letters R, D, and F. The patient should be given 60 seconds for each letter.
   Scoring:
   (1) Record the mean number of items recalled in a 60 second period. Score as follows: 5-15 words, 1 point; 15-25 words, 2 points; 25-35 words, 3 points; 35-45 words, 4 points; over 45 words, 5 points.
   (2) Note strategies automatically utilized by the patient – for example,

      (a) semantically similar words (daisy, daffodil, dandelion)
      (b) phonemically similar words (fan, fun, fin)
      (c) frequently occurring words,
      (d) identical final letters (fat, fit)
      (e) homonyms (do, dew)
      (f) changed second syllable (freshman, freshen, freshness) and identical initial blends (drink, drake)

g. Following oral directions (the patient is to wait until all instructions are given before responding):

   (1) Place picture of the sun, a dog, and a glass in front of the patient. When the patient is able to name each item, ask the patient to draw an X under the dog and a circle above the glass. Record the number of correct responses. (Total possible points: 1.)
   (2) Place a picture of a triangle, rectangle, circle, and square. When the patient is able to name each item, ask the patient to draw a line from the triangle to the rectangle that does not touch the circle or square. Record the number of correct responses. (Total possible points: 1.)
   (3) Place a paper on which the letters Q, T, S, R, M, B and D have been written in front of the patient. When the patient is able to name each letter, ask the patient to cross out the D, R, and letter after B, and put a circle around the S. Record the number of correct responses. (Total possible points: 1.)

difficult

h. Recall of a paragraph presented visually: Instruct the patient to read and verbally answer the questions that follow. Record the number of correct responses.

   (1) Many moths are serious pests. However, there are a few that are helpful to humans, such as the silkworm.

The silkworm is the chief source of commercial silk.
(a) Most moths are:
   very expensive   serious pests   used as pets
(b) The silkworm is the chief source of
   cocoons   cotton   silk
   (Total possible points: 2)
Tell me what you remember about the following paragraph:
The Bahama Islands are in the West Indies. They have a total area of 4400 square miles and a noted Tourist Center. In 1950, a vacation village was built in Nassau to accommodate the increased number of tourists. Tourists enjoy the climate and the water sports. There are numerous underwater attractions. The most popular of these is the underwater coral forest.
1. What is this story about?
2. How many square miles do the Bahama Islands cover?
3. Where was the vacation village built?
4. What do tourists enjoy?
5. What popular attraction are the tourists able to view underwater?
(Total possible points: 5)
i. Recall of a paragraph presented aurally: Read the following paragraphs to the patient and then ask the questions that pertain to the paragraph. Ask the patient to answer the questions verbally. Record the number of correct responses.
   (1) Arthur Middleton was a famous American artist. He was also a signer of the Declaration of Independence. He was later elected to the State Senate.
   (a) Who was this paragraph about?
   (b) What did he sign?
   (c) To what position was he later elected?
(Total possible points: 3)

   (2) A young man went to the store to buy a gift for his mother-in-law's birthday. He settled on a warm blue robe that cost $17.95. He thought that this would be appropriate as it was the winter season. The sales clerk folded the robe carefully and placed it in a bag. When he went to pay for the robe, the young man discovered he had only $15.25. The man was embarrassed. He decided to buy a pair of warm slippers for $11.00 and a key chain for $2.00. He left the store with change.
   (Total possible points: 4.)

(a) The man went to the store to buy a gift for his
wife   mother   mother-in-law
(b) The man wanted to buy something warm because

_____ He lived in a cold climate.
_____ It was almost winter.
_____ The person receiving the gift was ill
and often cold.
_____ The man was often cold.

(c) The man was embarrassed because
_____ The robe was too small.
_____ He did not have enough money.
_____ The sales clerk yelled at him.
_____ The robe wasn't warm enough.

(d) The man left the store with money in his pocket
because
_____ He paid with a credit card.
_____ He bought a cheaper gift.
_____ He decided not to buy a gift.
_____ He put the gift on layaway.

HIGH LEVEL THOUGHT PROCESSES

The purpose of this subtest is to assess high level problem solving, reasoning, and judgment. Specific areas tested include convergent thinking, deductive reasonings, inductive reasonings, divergent thinking, and multiprocess reasoning.

Convergent Thinking

Convergent thinking refers to recognition and analysis of relevant information to identify the central theme or main point.
After the patient has read the following information, ask him or her to verbally identify what the paragraph or sentences describe. Record the number of correct responses. (Total possible points: 3.)

1. Central theme identification
   a. Jack opened the door to his house and was greeted by a house full of people. The room was decorated with crepe paper and balloons and on the table sat a cake with candles. What is this story about?
   b. Walk to the booth, purchase a ticket, buy popcorn, take a seat, watch the screen.
      In what situation would you do the above?
   c. The man taps his foot nervously as he sits in the hard, un-

comfortable chair. As he turns and talks quietly with his lawyer, he appears to be unaware of the other people in the room. Soon a decision will be made.

What situation was described.

2. After the patient has read the first and third facts listed below, ask him or her to select the appropriate second missing fact in the list that follows. Record the correct responses. (Total possible points: 1.)

First fact: Kathy, who has a daughter age 17, is an 11th grade teacher at Mills Falls High School.

Second fact: Fact missing.

Third fact: Therefore, Kathy is a member of the Mills Falls High School PTA.

(a) Some teachers at Mills Falls High School are members of various professional organizations.

(b) All teachers at Mills Falls High School are members of the Mills Falls PTA.

(c) Parents of children attending high school can be members of the PTA.

(d) Teachers cannot have children attending the school where they teach.

Deductive Reasoning

Deductive reasoning is drawing conclusions based on premises or general principles in a step-by-step manner regarding a given situation.

1. After the patient has read all the clues below, ask him or her to select the correct item in the list of items that follows: (Total possible points: 1.)

can opener   iron   toaster   blender   coffeemaker

a. Does it open things?   No

b. Is it made of metal?   Yes

c. Does it become hot?   Yes

d. Is it used in the preparation of food?   No

2. After the patient has read the statement below, ask him or her to match the correct person with each vehicle using the clues that follow. Record the number of correct responses. (Total possible points: 4.)

Donna, Jim, Barb, and Tony each own a vehicle. These vehicles include a motorcycle, a small car, a truck, and a van.

(a) Tony carries large panes of glass, which must be cushioned on both sides.

(b) Donna has to haul large containers in her line of work.

    (c) Barb is able to take a short cut to work through a forest with dirt paths.

    (d) Donna's cargo must always be packed in waterproof containers as occasionally it gets wet during transport.

    (e) Jim's passenger door is broken at this time.

Inductive Reasoning

Inductive reasoning involves formulation of solutions based on details that lead to, but do not necessarily support, a standard conclusion.

1. Ask the patient to verbally provide the opposites of the following words, which are presented auditorially by the clinician. Record the number of correct responses. (Total possible points: 6.)

> full
> catch
> spoiled
> wild
> eliminate
> fragile

2. Ask the patient to provide a word that completes the following statements. The statements should be presented auditorially by the clinician. Record the number of correct responses. (Total possible points: 5.)

> _____Girl is to bed as baby is to _____.
> _____Pen is to author as seal is to_____.
> _____27 is to 29 as 33 is to _____.

Divergent Thinking

Divergent thinking involves generation of unique abstract concepts or hypotheses that deviate from standard concepts or ideas.

1. Homographs: Ask the patient to construct two sentences that depict two different meanings of the following words. Record the number of correct responses. (Total possible points: 4.)

> a. shoulder
> b. range

2. Idioms: Present the following idioms auditorially. Ask the patient to explain what each means. Require correct figurative meanings. (Total possible points: 3.)

> a. empty-headed
> b. bad egg
> c. heart of gold

3. Absurdities: Present the following absurdities auditorially. Ask the patient to explain what is absurd about each statement.

Record the number of correct responses. (Total possible points: 3.)

 a. The temperature rose to 25°F so he chipped through the ice and went for a swim.

 b. While out to dinner, a woman felt ill, so she asked the waiter to bring the dessert menu quickly.

 c. A young boy was having a difficult time moving a tall, heavy plant. He complained to his friend, "From now on I'm only going to move short plants."

4. Proverbs: Ask the patient to explain the following proverbs. Score the number of correct responses. (Total possible points: 2.)

 a. Don't count your chickens before they're hatched.

 b. People who live in glass houses shouldn't throw stones.

Multiprocess Reasoning

1. Task specific insight. Present the following situations to the patient. Ask the patient to answer the questions that follow. Record correct responses. The patient is to consider limitations due to disability and in his or her responses. Record the number of correct responses. (Total possible points: 7.)

 a. You are going on a shopping trip.

  (1) Name two things you will have to take with you.

  (2) How will you get there?

  (3) How many bags can you carry?

  (4) Will you need anyone to go with you?

 b. You are going to a doctor's appointment.

  (1) You're late; what will you do?

  (2) You have a flat tire; what will you do?

  (3) You don't understand instructions; what will you do?

 c. You're going to prepare a cup of instant coffee.

  (1) What special utensils will you need?

  (2) What will you do to compensate for your memory and organizational difficulties?

  (3) What are the steps you'll follow (i.e., what will you do first, second and so forth).

2. Ask the patient to decide whether there is too much information, too little information, or sufficient information to answer the following questions. Record the number of correct responses. (Total possible points: 3.)

 a. You just sold an article for 79 cents. What would you give the customer in addition to a dime to make exact change?

  (1) Not enough information.

  (2) Too much information.

  (3) Sufficient information.

b. Sara likes red, blue, and pink. She already has a red and blue sweater. But her slacks and shirts go best with red and blue. She just bought a skirt at her favorite store that would look best with a pink sweater. What color of sweater should she buy?

(1) Not enough information.
(2) Too much and unnecessary information.
(3) Sufficient information.

c. Mary weighs 190 lb. She needs to lose 52 lb. She does three different exercises each day: swimming, jogging, and bicycling. Swimming burns 13 calories per minute, jogging burns 15 calories per minute, and bicycling burns 3 calories per minute. In order to lose 1 lb., Mary must burn 3500 calories. How many days will it take her to lose this weight?

(1) Too little information.
(2) Too much and unnecessary information.
(3) Sufficient information.

Chapter 9

Cognitive Rehabilitation Techniques

Information processing, cognitive, and neurophysiological (attentional) deficits can be treated using a three-stage treatment hierarchy: arousal and alerting, operative retraining, and self-reliant functioning in the home and community. During the operative retraining phase of treatment, specific treatment areas include perception and attending, discrimination, organization, recall, and higher level thought processing (convergent thinking, deductive reasoning, inductive reasoning, divergent thinking, and multiprocess reasoning).

Although attempts have been made to order the tasks from easiest to most difficult, the hierarchy is somewhat arbitrary, and overlap can occur between the designated stages. It is often appropriate to work on the high-level tasks at one stage and the low-level tasks at the next stage.

GENERAL TREATMENT PROCEDURES

Treatment should focus on changing and modifying a patient's behavior, followed by the generalization of the behavior to the patient's home and community environments. To achieve this, the patient must be able to learn, retain, and generalize information. Learning a new fact requires the establishment and maintenance of new relationships or links between concepts that are already known. Patients with traumatic head injury have difficulty integrating, assimilating, or accommodating new information. Prior to initiating treatment, attempts should be made to determine each patient's premorbid functioning levels and behaviors that would influence treatment. Specific areas to be assessed include level of education, occupation, employment history, hobbies and interests, personality (e.g., introverted, extroverted), and style of learning. There are a variety of normal styles of learning, including visual or gestalt processing versus auditory or sequential processing; symbolic processing versus behavioral learning; structured or directive learning versus nonstructured or nondirective learning; and finally impulsive versus reflective responding.

Three general treatment states should be used with closed head injured patients, including stimulation or arousal and alerting, followed by structured, goal-oriented programs or operative retraining, and finally community-oriented programs or self-reliant functioning for residual cognitive deficits.

In the early stages of recovery, the clinician must direct efforts at eliciting and sustaining responses by the patient. All sensory modalities may be used (verbal, auditory, tactile, visual, cutaneous, olfactory, gustatory, and vestibular), and stimuli may be verbal or nonverbal. Clinicians must be flexible and search to discover the best methods of interaction and treatment for individual patients. For instance, a combination of tactile stimulation and verbal questioning may elicit some initial yes-no responses that are communicated with a subtle head nod or eye blink by certain patients. As the clinical picture evolves, the patient may begin to initiate more sustained communication. The clinician can then make use of these interactions as avenues to engage the patient in more advance therapy tasks. At the early stages, the purpose of treatment is to maximize potential responses in an appropriate therapeutic milieu. Early stimulation programs should include activities designed to excite patient activity. Next, attempts should be made to heighten or intensify these responses.

Intermediate or goal-oriented treatment stages should utilize activities designed to facilitate attention, perception, discrimination, organization, memory, and higher level problem analysis and problem solving. It is important that the complexity of tasks encountered in the therapy session is at a level that is appropriate for each patient. Each program must be tailored to the individual. The clinician must consider premorbid levels of functioning and behaviors and current cognitive abilities, sensorimotor limitations, and the presence of additional disorders, such as apraxia.

When designing therapy tasks, the clinician must define a skill, analyze all the segments or properties of the skill, develop a hierarchy of steps to accomplish the skill, plan techniques to achieve each step with consideration of the patient's style of learning, train the patient to a criterion as established for each segment along the hierarchy until the goal for target ability is reached, and finally evaluate the program continually and revise it when indicated. The clinician should begin with nonlinguistic stimuli that can be controlled for the physical features of color, shape, size, and so forth. The complexity of these tasks should be gradually increased by increasing the number of stimuli, the number of different dimensions of the stimuli (e.g., color, shape), and the rate and duration of stimulus presentation. When competency levels are achieved, linguistic stimuli should be introduced, and the clinician should move through a similar hierarchy with regard to task complexity. To initiate therapy, the clinician should select the area on the diagnostic and treatment continuum presented in Chapter 8 that is appropriate to the patient's level of information processing. Only when the client achieves success at that level should the next level be introduced. To avoid frustration, the client should not be required to participate in tasks which are beyond his or her ability level. In order for structured tasks to be meaningful to the patient, the clinician should relate structured therapy tasks to functional environmental activities—for example, sequencing tasks are necessary if the patient is to become independent in activities of daily living, such as cooking, making a cup of coffee, and washing clothes. Maintaining continuity from session to session, establishing goals with patient input, and charting progress daily for patient review are important.

Higher level cognitive tasks require individuals to be active processors of information. Problem solving in general occurs in several stages. First, an attempt must be made to understand or analyze the problem. Next, a person must devise a solution, a strategy, and several alternatives based on past experiences stored in long-term memory. The solution is executed and, finally, the solution must be evaluated. The ability to solve problems requires the mental shifting of attention across many variables, with occasional reference to the initial instructions. In these later steps, the ability to perform in an environment with an increasing number of distractions is necessary. During cognitive rehabilitation, stimuli should be introduced to increase the tolerance to distraction. The ability to encode information concisely and the ability to self-correct hypotheses once given feedback should also be included at more advanced levels. Vallier and Wertz (1978) suggested that the clinician's role with closed head injured patients is to help the patient recognize cognitive and affective disorders and to help him or her intellectualize those deficits that are amenable to compensatory strategies. Bower (1978) suggested, as a human being learns, he or she becomes aware of the contingencies and only then begins to respond appropriately, provided that there is motivation to do so. "Figuring out the contingencies" means becoming aware of and being able to recognize the stimulus-action-outcome correlations that are programmed into the situation. After designing situations of increasing levels of difficulty, the clinician can initially provide dues to facilitate contingency and recognition. The use of cues should then be gradually faded. There is an increasing demand on attention and recall as tasks become more difficult. These behaviors should be, therefore, a secondary focus of every therapy task. An individual is unable to move to more difficult cognitive levels in the treatment hierarchy without improvements in these areas.

Lerner specified five questions that must be answered in analyzing a task: (1) what does a task require in terms of receptive and expressive abilities; (2) what type of sensory involvement does the patient have; (3) what is the nature of tasks (verbal or nonverbal); (4) what are the social and nonsocial contributions of the tasks; and (5) what skills are required in performing the task, and how does the patient's cognitive disabilities involve these skills? Additional therapy task considerations include an assessment of the number of responses required at any one time; allowances for some degree of initial success; and the use of redundancy.

Ben-Yishay (1978) suggested that compensation hypothesis is a plausible explanation of the beneficial effects of cognitive remediation with closed head injured patients such that the clinician should attempt to identify strategies used spontaneously by the patient and should gear treatment toward the expanded use of these strategies. When simplified or inappropriate strategies are used by the patient, the clinician should attempt to demonstrate the inadequacy of the strategy using the following steps: (1) present the task and record the errors; (2) generate an hypothesis concerning the nature of the oversimplified strategies, such as watching the sequence of motor and eye movements as the patient executes the task, or determining if there is a modified problem or a reduced set of information for which the patient's answers could be correct; (3) gather data that will permit a choice to be made among strategies if more than one strategy might underlie patient's errors; (4) once the strategy used by the patient spontaneously is identified, specify it as a series of steps unfolding in time, such as in the writing of a computer program.

Parrill-Burnstein (1981) suggested the following guidelines for clinicians during compensatory treatment: (1) assess client's use of strategies; (2) institute continuous reinforcement schedules; (3) present verbal and nonverbal cues simultaneously, but not as competing cues; and (4) apply task analysis procedures when designing training procedures. When remediating problems, clinicians can focus on instructions in different ways, depending on their philosophical orientation. Skills can be taught by focusing on learning integrities, focusing on the deficits, or using the learning strengths or integrities in remediation of the learning deficits. The latter position was first suggested by Johnson and Myklebust (1967) and is referred to as the two-pronged approach. The rationale for the two-pronged approach is as follows: If the patient is taught only to use learning strengths, the gap or discrepancy between the learning deficits in those integrities increases, but if training focuses on the deficit areas, the patient's frustration may compound the learning difficulties. Working the learning integrities or strengths into a lesson for remediation of the deficits in performance, however, may result in faster acquisition with less failure and frustration.

Patient motivation is extremely important. A "motive" is roughly a valued goal plus a plan to achieve it. When a person commits himself or herself to carrying out a plan, he or she has an intention to do so. As a plan is executed and the cost versus value and success are evaluated, the individual may choose to alter the goal or may choose another plan. The underlying structure of behavioral events is a hierarchical, organized sequence of actions composing a goal-directed plan or episodes. Most events people experience in everyday life involve people carrying out goal-directed activity. An observer can usually only recognize another's plans by knowing what the person wants and what the person believes about the world (Bower, 1978).

The final phase of therapy, or the carryover phase, should be geared toward the carryover of treatment goals to functional home and community situations. Home and community training within and outside the hospital provides opportunities for the practice of necessary skills and often serves to lessen denial of deficits. Multidisciplinary group therapy is especially beneficial during this stage. Specific group therapy information is provided later in this chapter.

AROUSAL AND ALERTING

Initially, attempt to activate a response to any stimulus (tactile, auditory, visual, verbal, gustatory, olfactory, or vestibular), and gradually increase the frequency, type, and duration of the response. Arousal and alerting tends to be dependent on the strength of the stimulus. When presenting the stimuli, work through one modality at a time. Sensory deprivation must be avoided and abnormal reflexes must be decreased, although treatment initially focuses on the elicitation of reflexes. Most stimulation programs are completed by several disciplines, including Occupation and Physical Therapy, Speech-Language Pathology, and Nursing.

Specific activities include the following:

1. Auditory stimulation and tracking tasks that progress from the use of gross, nonspeech sounds (bells, buzzers, musical instruments) to more finely discriminated speech sounds. Begin with both live and taped familiar voices of family members and progress to unfamiliar voices, including those on the radio and television.

2. Oral peripheral stimulation, including passive stretching and the use of facilitative exercises for increasing the range of the articulators (e.g., licking a lollipop or placing food at the corner of the mouth for tongue control, or using a straw for lip control).

3. Verbal stimulation in which gross, reflexive sounds are elicited first. Work toward vocalizations appropriate to specific situations. A listing of suppliers of recommended therapy materials is provided at the end of this chapter.

4. Tactile stimulation using a variety of textures (feather, sand paper, tongue blade, cotton swab, oral hygiene swab, hand, and so forth) and temperatures to various parts of the body, including the lips, tongue, and oral cavity.

5. Visual stimulation using bright lights, colors, familiar pictures, and familiar objects (such as calendars, clocks, personal grooming items).

6. Gustatory stimulation using foods that include bitter, sour, sweet, salt, and bland flavors.

7. Olfactory stimulation beginning with strong noxious smells (e.g., ammonia, sulfur) followed by strong pleasant smells (e.g., perfume, coffee) and finally external environmental smells.

8. Vestibular stimulation is best accomplished in physical therapy and occupational therapy sessions using techniques typically used with sensory impaired children.

PERCEPTION AND ATTENDING

Basic attentional skills are necessary for patients to actively participate in therapy sessions. Attentional skills must also continue to improve as the patient progresses through the treatment continuum. Improvement in attentional skills is, therefore, a secondary focus of every task. Initially, attempts should be made to initiate and sustain attention for brief periods. The stimuli and environment should be highly controlled by the clinician, with the presentation of one stimulus at a time. Next, attempts should be made to extend the length of time the patient is capable of maintaining attention. An additional goal is the appropriate shifting of attention from one item to another.

Specific therapy activities include visual and auditory tasks in which

1. The patient is asked to track an auditory stimulus or scan a visual stimulus (such as a line).

2. The patient is asked to perceive and recognize environmental sounds and words and point to the corresponding pictures.

3. The patient is asked to trace or copy a figure followed by words.

4. The patient is required to draw within boundaries (i.e.,

_____

_____).

5. The patient is to bisect lines by drawing a line through the midpoint of the horizontal lines. Begin with one line per page and gradually add more lines.

6. The patient is asked to follow simple commands (e.g., "open your eyes," "close your mouth").

Examples of published therapy materials (see list of Source Materials at the end of the chapter):

1. Keith: *Speech and Language Rehabilitation,* Vol. I.
   Copying words (pp. 19-52)
2. *Therapy Guide for the Adult with Language and Speech Disorders, Vol. I.*
   Automatic Activities (pp. 193, 250, 169-171)
   Copying Activities (pp. 231-251)
3. *Life Science Associates:* Computer Software
   REACT
   Speeded Reading Word Lists
4. *Psychological Software Services:* Computer Software
   Foundation Skills
   Visuospatial Skills

DISCRIMINATION

Discrimination is a process during which two or more stimuli are differentiated. During selective attention, the patient must discriminate multiple aspects of a stimulus situation at any moment in time. Irrelevant and extraneous stimuli must be determined. It is important to note that the salient or pertinent aspects might or might not be related to the strengths or intensity of the stimulus as in the arousal attentional phase. During the selective attention process, the patient must rely on contextual cues. The threshold for highly pertinent information must be continually adjusted. This establishment of pertinence becomes a cognitive and not a sensory process. The adjustment is based on existing inputs and expectations of future inputs and requires perceptual and discrimination skills.

Treatment must focus on gradually increasing the number and degree of similarity of alternative stimuli that compete with the most pertinent stimuli. Daily activities require selective attention in which multiple aspects of a stimulus situation must be discriminated at any moment in time. The patient must now be able to initiate, sustain, and switch attention from one stimulus to another. Relevant, irrelevant, and extraneous stimuli must be identified. It is important to note that the salient or pertinent aspects of a stimulus are not necessarily related to the strength or intensity of the stimulus, as in the arousal or alerting activities. During discrimination selective attention is required in which the patient must rely on contextual cues. The threshold for highly pertinent information must be continually adjusted.

Specific therapy activities include visual and auditory tasks in which:

1. The patient is given a "connect the dots" task varying in degree of difficulty, beginning with two dots and increasing to an unlimited number in a complex pattern.

2. The patient is to discriminate color, shape, or size by visually matching geometric forms or by pointing to the forms in response to an auditory command. Initially show only two response items, which differ by only one feature (e.g., same shape, same size, different colors). Gradually, the number of items and the features per response set should be increased.

3. The patient is to visually match objects to objects, followed by pictures to pictures, letters to letters, words to words, and words to objects. Gradually increase the complexity of the response set by increasing the number of items and the degree of color, shape, size, and function similarities of the response items (e.g., match a pen to a pen in an array of objects, including pencil, magic marker, chalk, and pen).

4. The patient is required to point to objects, pictures, letters, and words when identified by name. Begin with a field of two items and gradually increase the number as well as the phonemic and semantic similarity of the response items.

5. The patient is to cancel or cross out a specified letter in a string of letters going from left to right on a page. The clinician

should gradually add more lines of letters per page.

6. The patient is required to visually match a picture to a sentence. Begin with a field of two items and gradually increase the number of response items.

7. The patient must auditorially discriminate between words or sentences. When given two visually or auditorially similar words (e.g., cat and cot) or sentences (e.g., she picked up the dog or she picked at the dog), the patient is to correctly identify the word or sentence given verbally by the clinician.

Examples of published therapy materials:

1. *Modern Education Corporation*
   Auditory Discrimination Game
2. *Therapy Guide for the Adult with Language and Speech Disorders*
   Point to Objects (p. 9)
   Body Parts Match to Words (p. 12)
   Point to Letters (p. 14)
   Point to Word from Choice (pp. 15, 16)
   Sentences Matching to Pictures (pp. 24-26)
   Matching Objects (pp. 65, 70)
   Matching Letters (p. 67)
   Matching Words (pp. 68, 69)
   Matching Words to Pictures (pp. 71-74)
   Matching Pictures to Sentences (pp. 86-89)
3. *The Thinking Skills Workbook: A Cognitive Skills Remediation Manual for Adults*
   Cross Out the Letters (p. 12)
   Cross Out/Match Letters (pp. 36-40)
   Match Letters/Symbols (pp. 41, 42)
   Cross Out Same Letter (pp. 43, 44)
   Find Word in Group of Words (pp. 51-54)
   Find Word in Group of Letters (pp. 57-60, 63-72)
4. *Developmental Learning Materials*
   Visual Discrimination Flip Book I – Pictures
   Visual Discrimination Flip Book II – Shapes
5. *Brain Link Computer Software*
   Word Recognition I, II, III
   Color I and II
6. *Compu-tations, Inc.:* Computer Software
   Color Match – Early Elementary I
   Shape Match
7. *Edu-Ware Services, Inc.:* Computer Software
   Shape Recognition

Size Comparison
8. *Laureate Learning Systems:* Computer Software
First Words
9. *Life Science Associates:* Computer Software
Search

ORGANIZATION

The process of organization plays an important role in the acquisition of new information, in recall, and in other high-level processes, such as problem solving and logical thinking. The organization of information utilizes learned strategies in which discrete actions or components of stimuli must be organized and sequenced according to the priority of each component. Six types of organizational tasks are presented here, including categorization, closure, sequencing, fragmented stimuli, figure ground, and daily routines.

Specific therapy tasks used to improve organization skills include the following:

Categorization

Categorization tasks are those in which the patient is first required to identify optimal categories, recognize subtle differences, and then switch sets. These include the following:

1. The patient is to visually sort, or give to the clinician upon request, a group of geometric forms by sizes, shapes, and colors. Begin with four items that differ by only one feature (e.g., same size, same color, different shapes) and gradually increase the number of items and stimulus features in each response set.

2. The patient must match items (pictures, letters, words, and so forth) that are in the same class but are not identical (e.g., match A to a, or match different species of birds).

3. The patient is to sort objects when the categorical set is changed and the same objects are used (e.g., a group of geometric forms first are sorted according to color, then according to shape, then according to size).

4. Discuss attributes of various geometric shapes (i.e., number of sides, angles, horizontal lines). Give the patient additional shapes, which must be assigned to specific groups based on similarities and differences to other group members.

5. Present the patient with two equal quantities of clay formed into different shapes (i.e., ball versus cigar shape). The patient is required to evaluate whether or not the same amount of clay was used. This same task can be done with liquids and other solids (discrimination of quantity concepts).

6. Arbitrarily assign nonsense names to several groups of geometric shapes. The similar and different attributes of each group must be analyzed by the patient in order to assign names to new stimuli presented by the clinician.

7. The patient is required to sort objects into general categories, such as food, eating utensils, or writing implements. Items should then be subdivided into more specific categories, such as fruits, vegetables, meats.

8. The patient is asked to sort picture cards or objects according to various traits (i.e., function, size, color).

9. Given a group activity picture or a heavily detailed picture, the patient is to ask a variety of detailed questions to determine what object in the picture is the target stimulus (e.g., What is its color? What is its function?).

10. The patient is asked to give a response that is not part of or is different from a particular category situation or context. A category exclusion task would be to have the patient name something that he or she would eat that is not hot. A situation exclusion task would be to ask the patient to name something he or she would not wear skiing. A context exclusion task would be to require the patient to name something he or she should not do at an opera.

11. The patient is to verbally provide descriptive (physical attributes) and functional (uses) similarities and differences between two objects, such as a table and a chair or an orange and a cantaloupe.

12. The patient is asked to identify a variety of items that would be needed in a given situation (e.g., for taking a bath, the patient would identify soap, sponge, and so forth). This is a necessary step prior to sequencing the steps of taking a bath.

Closure Activities

1. Nonlinguistic tasks are presented that require the identification of geometric forms with sections missing – for example:

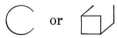

Next, pictures are presented of objects with parts missing and scenes with objects missing.

2. Visual linguistic tasks are presented that require the identification of words with portions of letters missing (e.g., si\ ); words with letters missing (last letter should be omitted first, followed by initial letter, then medial letters – e.g., lak__, __ake,

l__ke, b__tt__m); sentences with words missing (e.g., John _____ to the store); steps to the completion of a task with one or more steps missing; and paragraphs with sentences missing.

3. Auditory linguistic tasks are presented, such as sound blending, in which phonemes are individually presented, and the patient must identify the word.

Sequencing Tasks

1. Nonlinguistic tasks are presented requiring the patient to sequence a color from light to dark shades or objects from small to large.

2 . Linguistic tasks are presented requiring the patient to do the following:

   a. Connect dots in a numerical or alphabetical order.

   b. Reorder (forward and backward) strings of numbers, letters, days of week, and months of the year.

   c. Visually or auditorially sequence words in which letters or syllables are out of order, sentences in which words are scrambled, and paragraphs in which sentences are scrambled.

   d. Sequence steps of activities of daily living, including washing, eating, shopping, and so forth.

   e. Match numbers with corresponding letters of a code and then break the code (e.g., if 1 = A, 2 = B, 3 = C, then what is 3-1-2?

   f. Follow written directions of increasing complexity (e.g., circle every /e/ in the first and second words of a sentence).

   g. Follow written directions for filling out forms, following a recipe, understanding a map, and so forth.

   h. Give directions to another person for how to move from one point in the clinic to another.

   i. First organize geometric shapes into a design (i.e.,). The patient must then give the clinician step-by-step directions to reproduce the design on the other side of a barrier (e.g., first put the blue circle in the middle, put the one corner of the red triangle above and to the left, with one corner touching the blue circle, and so forth).

Fragmented Stimuli

1. The patient is to correctly assemble stimulus items, such as pictures of common objects, which are cut into pieces.

2. The patient is to correctly assemble puzzles. Begin with simple puzzles and progress to more complex ones.

Figure Ground Tasks

Figure ground tasks are those in which questions must be answered regarding information presented aurally under various conditions of background noise (e.g., cafeteria conversation, traffic sounds).

Daily Routines

Daily routines, such as treatment schedules, placement of articles in the room, and functional tasks (e.g., washing, dressing, cooking, money management, shopping) should be organized. Initially order in the patient's environment should be provided; but the patient should gradually accept the responsibility for establishing this order. A treatment schedule should be prepared by the patient. Articles in the room should be categorized according to function, and the steps of each functional task should be identified and sequenced.

Examples of published therapy materials for organizational tasks:

1. *Developmental Learning Materials*
   Shopping Lists – Game II
   Association Picture Cards I-IV
   Career Association Cards
   Category Cards
2. *Teaching Resources*
   People, Places, Things
   Touring America
   Categories – Food and Animals
   Alike Because, Level I and Level 2
   Categories: Clothing and Household Items
   Associations, Sets 1 and 2
   Categories: Varied
3. *Basic Thinking Skills*
   Associations, Set I and II
   Verbal Classifications
   Similarities and Differences
   Patterns
4. *Language Remediation Workbook*
   Categories and Classification (pp. 113-122)

RETRIEVAL

Retrieval or recall of information depends on the following abilities: initiate, sustain, and switch attention; recognize relevant and irrelevant information; rehearse, organize, and store information; and recall information in an organized manner. If any of these steps break down, information to be retrieved may be unavailable.

Before the retrieval strategies outlined in this section are introduced, the patient must achieve competency levels in previous states of the treatment continuum, including arousal and alerting, perception and attending, discrimination, and organization of information.

Auditory and visual retention hierarchies are based on the length and amount of information that must be processed, organized, and recalled. Tasks should progress from single items (geometric forms, letters, numbers, and words) to phrases and short sentences followed by stories and situations. Within each task, item complexity can be increased by considering the following: abstract items are more difficult to recall than concrete items; similar items are more difficult to recall than dissimilar items; and unfamiliar and non-meaningful information is more difficult to recall than familiar, meaningful information.

Teaching rehearsal strategies or techniques that facilitate the storage and recall of information should be the primary forms of treatment.

Specific retrieval strategies include the following:

1. Verbal description, in which an adequate explanation of items, concepts, and so forth, to be recalled is provided by the patient or clinician. In therapy, visual, auditory, and semantic descriptions should be encouraged.

2. Visual imagery, in which objects, scenes of a story or situation, and maps of layouts in space are mentally pictured.

3. Chunking activities, in which information is organized into segments that coincide with the patient's memory span (e.g., if the patient can recall only two items, information should be divided into two-item segments). When possible, meaningful units should be considered when chunking information. When memory is organized into chunks, retrieval of one unit or chunk of information will provide access to more than a single item owing to the relationship of the items in the unit. To accomplish chunking, stimuli can be separated into segments visually by using different colors or sizes for each segment. During aural presentation of stimuli, the segments can be presented using different loudnesses or pitches. The segments can also be physically separated during visual or auditory presentation of the information.

4. Categorization of information to improve recall of that information (e.g., when required to remember 15 items to be purchased at a grocery store, the patient should group the items into categories such as dairy products, frozen foods, meats).

5. Rehearsal, in which information to be recalled is drilled. Verbal repetition is used; the information is repeated first aloud, then subvocally by mouthing the words, and finally silently. Visually, the patient can continually review the details of visual images or written stimuli. Requiring the patient to maintain a daily log of events provides for rehearsal of activities occurring daily and weekly.

6. Associations, in which relationships between items or events to be stored or recalled are recognized and accentuated. Associations can be based on semantic relationships (e.g., cane-crutches and day-night), acoustic relationships (dew-shoe), or visual relationships (desk-dresser).

7. Temporal or spatial ordering, in which events in episodic and semantic memory are recalled by remembering certain landmark events associated with the event to be recalled or those that occurred at a similar point in time. Actions or events can often be recalled if the goals or results of the action are recalled. Initially, emphasize key events during encoding. Using selective reminding during recall, question and cue patients regarding key events. Gradually the number of cues should be reduced.

8. Primacy and recency benefits, in which the first or last item is recalled more often than central items in a string of items. To increase the effects of primacy and recency, the first and last items in a string should be accented visually using different colors and sizes, or auditorially, using different loudnesses and pitches.

9. Mnemonic devices, in which specific memory tricks are used to increase associative learning through paired association. During encoding, new words or bits of information are chained or paired to a preestablished set of key words and phrases or a familiar sequence of known locations.

The following tasks can be utilized to teach one or several of the strategies:

1. The patient is shown figures, objects, or words on cards. The cards are then placed face down and the patient is asked to point to the location of a specific stimulus.

2. An array of objects, figures, or words is placed before the patient. The patient is asked to remember all of the objects. While the patient is turned away, one or several objects are removed. The patient is then requested to recall the missing objects.

3. Paragraphs of varying lengths are auditorially or visually presented, after which the patient is asked yes-no or multiple choice questions.

4. The patient is presented with a series of commands, which can be carried out in the immediate surroundings (e.g., "Pick up the pencil, put in on the desk, close the book, and turn your chair around"). The patient is encouraged to visualize the space, stimuli, and actions as the commands are given. A series of commands are then given that involve areas or persons not immediately visible (e.g., "Go to the nursing station for a piece of paper and stop at your room for a glass"). Again, the patient is asked to visualize the

stimuli and actions as the directions are presented.

5. The patient is asked to look at a detailed picture in the newspaper and to read the corresponding article. The patient is then asked a variety of questions concerning the details of the article and the picture.

6. The patient is presented with a message to be delivered to a specific person at the end of the day.

HIGH LEVEL THOUGHT PROCESSES

When teaching cognitive skills, a demonstration and description, rather than solely description, should be provided. This technique is particularly important if language skills are impaired. High level cognitive tasks require the patient to be an active processor of information. Problem solving or reasoning occurs in several stages; a person must first attempt to understand or analyze the problem; a solution, a strategy, and several alternatives (hypotheses) are then formulated based on past experiences stored in long-term memory; a solution is generated or executed; and finally, the solution is evaluated. During problem-solving tasks, head trauma patients tend to have a narrow perspective, which results in a concrete and incomplete analysis of problems. They do not take time to think through problems. Patients also have difficulty deciding how to approach the problem. Their ability to generate hypotheses and employ strategies is reduced. The need for additional information is not recognized, and solutions, therefore, are based on incomplete or partial information.

Treatment should focus on a variety of problem-solving strategies. When teaching problem-solving techniques, begin by leading the patient through each step in the process, using visual and verbal cues. Next, cues should be provided only when necessary to keep the patient on target. Finally, the patient is to solve the problem independently. When planning therapy, present convergent or analytical thinking skills first, followed by deductive reasoning tasks, inductive reasoning tasks, and finally divergent thinking tasks.

Convergent Thinking

During convergent thinking tasks, the patient analyzes information in order to identify the central or main point. This process requires recognition of relevant and irrelevant information. In communicative situations, convergent thinking skills allow an individual to understand and formulate the general theme of a conversation, situation or written article.

Specific therapy tasks include the following:

1. The identification of a common theme in a group of objects (i.e., shoes and bread—both have heels).

2. The identification of one word that could be combined with four other words to form another set of words, e.g. saddle, stroke, track, and show could all be combined with the word side (sidesaddle, sidestroke, and so forth).

3. The generalization of details to come up with a common situation or place (e.g., given the sentence "You look for wood, you put up your tent, you set up the picnic table, you catch your dinner," the patient is to identify the situation. Another example would be "He sits in the chair, the technician cleans his teeth, he has x-rays taken of his mouth").

4. The identification of relevant information in visually or auditorially presented sentences, paragraphs, and conversations with respect to who did what, when, and where. The Folkes Sentence Builder series is helpful for this task.

5. The reduction of information to the most salient items by abstracting the main idea of visually or auditorially presented sentences, paragraphs, and conversations. Key facts and situations should be identified by considering the intent of the sender and the interpretation of the receiver.

Examples of published therapy materials:

1. *Therapy Guide for the Adult with Language and Speech Disorders, Vol. I.*
   Who, What, Where Activity (pp. 122, 123)
   Paragraphs Central Theme (pp. 211, 212)
2. *Therapy Guide for the Adult with Language and Speech Disorders, Vol. II*
   Given Clues, Come Up with Conclusion (pp. 24-27)
3. *Manual of Exercises for Expressive Reasoning*
   Interpolative Thinking (pp. 103-109)
4. *Brubaker Workbook for Aphasia*
   Why, What, When, Where, Who, How Questions (pp. 237-248)
5. *Teachers College Press*
   Gates-Peardon Reading Exercises
6. *Reader's Digest Skill Builders and Advanced Skill Builders*
7. *Teaching Resources*
   What's Wrong Here? Level I and Level II
8. *Teaching Resources*
   Fokes Sentence Builder
9. Davidson and Associates: Computer Software
   Multiple Choice Quiz—Word Attach

10. *Edu-Ware Services, Inc.:* Computer Software
    Sentences
11. *Sunset Software:* Computer Software
    Understanding Questions
    Understanding Sentences

Deductive Reasoning

Deductive reasoning is a process in which conclusions are drawn from given data or situations based on premises or general principles. This requires an analysis that progresses from the whole situation to specific parts or features. Deductive reasoning is necessary in linguistic and nonlinguistic problem-solving tasks, which requires an individual to form conclusions supported by the information given. Specific therapy tasks include the following:

1. Forward or backward chaining, in which the patient is to deal with the relevant information and devise solutions in a progressive (forward) or regressive (backward) step-by-step process until the final solution is reached. Problems are presented in Mind Benders: Deductive Thinking Skills (*Basic Thinking Skills*), which require a forward process of variable elimination. Situational pictures can be given that require a backward process of variable elimination (e.g., a picture of an accident involving two cars).

2. Missing premise tasks, in which two facts are necessary to reach a conclusion. If given one fact, the patient is to choose the second fact that leads to the conclusion (e.g., given "All children must go to school and Bob and Jane are children," the patient is to deduce that Bob and Jane must go to school). The Ross Test of Higher Cognitive Processes is especially useful for these tasks.

3. Analysis of sentences and paragraphs to determine punctuation, spelling, and other grammatical errors.

Examples of published therapy materials:

1. *Basic Thinking Skills*
   Mind Benders Series: A1-A3, B1-B4, C1-C3
   Word Benders Series
   Think About It
   What Would You Do? And True to Life or Fantasy?
2. *Brubaker Workbook for Aphasia*
   Making Conclusions (pp. 259-266)
3. *Manual of Exercises for Expressive Reasoning*
   Determining Missing Information (pp. 113-118)
4. *Practice In Survival Reading: Books 2-8*
   Book 2, Signs Around Town

Book 3, Label Talk
Book 4, Read the Instructions First
Book 5, It's on the Map
Book 7, Let's Look it Up
Book 8, Caution, Find Print Ahead
5. *The Amazing Adventures of Harvey Crumbaker—Skills for Living*
6. *Computer-Advanced Ideas, Inc.:* Computer Software
The Game Show
7. *Minnesota Educational Computing Consortium:* Computer Software
Oregon
Voyageur
8. *Program Design, Inc.:* Computer Software
Number Power I-V
9. *Slossen Educational Publications, Inc.*
Ross Test of Higher Cognitive Processes

Inductive Reasoning

Inductive reasoning is a process in which solutions are formulated by considering particular details that lead to, but do not necessarily support, a general conclusion. This requires an analysis of parts or details to formulate an overall, or whole, concept. In communication situations, a person must analyze given details and gather additional information in order to assess a situation—for example, in determining whether a call should be placed to the rescue squad, a person must gather information to judge the seriousness of the situation. Specific therapy tasks include the following:

1. The formulation of antonyms and synonyms. Crossword puzzles are useful in this task.

2. Analogous thinking, in which the patient is given two or more items or pairs of items that must be analyzed with regard to similar or different features to provide a word or pair of words related in the same way (e.g., the patient is to respond "cat" if given the statement, "Bark is to dog as meow is to ____").

3. Cause and effect tasks, in which either the cause or the effect of a situation is presented. The patient must indicate the appropriate solution (e.g., if given, "Boiling water is spilled on a woman's hand," the patient is to indicate that the woman's hand is burned; or if given "A woman's hand is burned," the patient is to indicate that the woman's hand came in contact with a source of heat such as boiling water or fire).

4. The patient is asked to describe what facial expression or emotion would be appropriate in a particular situation (e.g., what emo-

tion would be appropriate if your wallet was stolen?).

5. Open-ended problem solving, including story completion tasks, in which the patient is required to complete an unfinished story.

6. Decision-making tasks, in which a situation is given and the patient is required to make a choice between possible solutions (e.g., if given the problem "John needs money," the patient is to indicate that John should go to work rather than rob a bank or choose other possible, but socially unacceptable, solutions). Next the patient must generate his or her own solution (e.g., the patient is told that he has a doctor's appointment and his car won't start. What should he do?).

7. The patient is asked to develop solution sets by responding to wh-questions (e.g., "Why do cars have wheels?" or "Why couldn't you wear shoes swimming?").

8. After reading an article or listening to a situation presented by the clinician, the patient is to be given an opinion statement.

Examples of published therapy materials:
1. *Inductive Thinking Skills*
   Verbal Classifications
   Cause and Effect
   Relevant Information
   Inferences: A and B
   Reasoning by Analogies
   Antonyms and Synonyms
   Analogies: A-D
   Open-ended Problems
   Antonyms, Synonyms, Similarities, and Differences
2. *Manual of Exercises for Expressive Reasoning*
   Wh- Questions (pp. 69-76)
   Predicting Outcome (pp. 79-87)
   Predicting Comparatively (pp. 88-94)
   Making Inferences (pp. 121-132)
   Identifying Causes of an Event (pp. 135-140)
   Role Projection (pp. 151-158)
   Criticizing (pp. 177-180)
3. *Developmental Learning Materials*
   Antonym Cards
   Word Master
4. *Language Remediation Workbook*
   Analogies
   Antonyms

Homophones
5. *Therapy Guide for the Adult with Language and Speech Disorders, Vol. I*
   Sentence Completion (pp. 83-85)
   Word Associations (pp. 95, 247-248)
   Synonyms (p. 115)
   Opposites (pp. 116-117, 172, 207, 251)
   Cause and Effect Relationship (pp. 207, 208, 262)
6. *Brubaker Workbook for Aphasia*
   Antonyms (pp. 15-26)
   Homonyms (pp. 27-40)
7. *The Thinking Skills Workbook: A Cognitive Skills Remediation Manual for Adults*
   Decision Making Tasks (pp. 195-197)
8. *Therapy Guide for the Adult with Language and Speech Disorders, Vol. II*
   Word Associations (pp. 23, 66-67)
   Analogies (pp. 128, 129)
   Cause and Effect, (pp. 37, 76, 77)
   Story Completion, (pp. 41-54)
   Decision Making Tasks (pp. 5-9, 57-60, 64, 65, 73-76, 79, 80, 130, 131, 128, 143)
   Synonyms, (p. 91)
   Opposites (p. 92)
   Sentence Completion (pp. 95-97)
9. *Edu-Ware Services, Inc.:* Computer Software
   Synonyms and Antonyms
   PSAT Prefixes
10. *Program Design, Inc.:* Computer Software
    Vocabulary: Opposites I - IV
    Vocabulary: Synonyms I - III
    Vocabulary Quiz
11. *University Park Press:* Computer Software
    Aphasia Therapy II

Divergent Thinking

Divergent thinking results in the generation of unique abstract concepts or hypotheses that deviate from standard concepts or ideas. The hypotheses or concepts must then be tested. Without divergent thinking skills, linguistic and situational paradoxes, abstractions, and subtleties are overlooked, and experiences are often viewed incorrectly owing to literal or concrete interpretations. Specific therapy tasks include the following:

1. Multimeaning stimuli (homographs), in which the patient is required to construct sentences depicting several meanings for each sentence or phrase (e.g., given the word "shoulder," responses could be "A shoulder is part of your body," "He drove on the shoulder of the road," or "You don't have to shoulder the burden").

2. Multifunction stimuli (simile and metaphor formulation and interpretation) requiring the analysis of a figure of speech in which one object or event is described in terms usually denoting another object or event (e.g., "the ship plowed the sea"). A likeness or analogy between the objects or events is implied, although abstract thinking is required to discern the similarities.

3. The patient is required to respond to "realism" questions, (e.g., "Is a bigger tree also an older tree?" or "If you didn't have that name, would you still be the same person?").

4. Absurdities, in which the patient is to describe what is absurd about statements, stories, or pictures (e.g., when given "The temperature rose to 25°, so he chipped through the ice and went for a swim," the patient is to identify the absurdity and correct the statement).

5. Idiom interpretation, requiring the patient to provide explanations of phrases in which the meaning generally cannot be derived from the literal interpretation of its parts (e.g., empty-headed, chicken-hearted, clear as mud, on pins and needles).

6. Proverb interpretations, requiring the patient to analyze a statement in which true, nonstandard abstract meanings and relationships of items are given. The statements can be satirical or paradoxical as well as contraindicatory or nonsensical. These truths are of a general rather than specific nature.

7. The interpretation of poetry, fables, puns, jokes, and riddles, which requires the patient to consider abstract relations, double meanings, paradoxes, and nonstandard meanings.

Examples of published therapy materials:
1. *Teaching Resources*
   What's Wrong Here? Level I and Level II
   Visual Absurdities
2. *Language Remediation Workbook*
   Idioms (pp. 74-77)
   Absurd Sentences (p. 131-133)
   Similes (p. 73)
3. *Therapy Guide for the Adult with Language and Speech Disorders, Vol. I*
   Multimeaning Words (p. 199)

Multiprocess Reasoning

Multiprocess reasoning requires the use of two or more of the processes described previously. Specific therapy tasks include the following:

1. Determining whether sufficient, insufficient, or extra and unnecessary information has been provided in a given problem. If the information is inadequate to solve the problem, the patient must use a questioning strategy to gather necessary information regarding the central features of the problem.

2. Responding to questions based on an analysis of syllogisms or arguments consisting of a major and a minor premise and a conclusion—e.g., given the following assumptions: (a) If John catches a 5 pound fish, he will win a trophy, (b) If John wins two more trophies this month, he will have won a total of six trophies, (c) John does not catch a 5 pound fish. The patient is to answer the questions: (a) Did John win a trophy? (b) Could John win six trophies during this month? Using deductive reasoning, a conclusion is derived by the patient based on the two or more assumptions. In the second, more complex, part of this task, the validity of the conclusion must be determined by means of inductive reasoning. The patient must determine the need for additional information based on an analysis of the pertinent details. The Syllogisms: If-Then Statements Series (*Midwest Publications*) provides useful stimuli for these tasks.

3. The mediation of an argument requiring analysis and synthesis of information. Two points of view in a specific argument should be presented. Using deductive reasoning, the premises or assumptions of each person must be considered in order to arrive at a solution. Once this is accomplished, the solution must be tested by analyzing the truth of the premises. Finally, utilizing complementary reasoning, a compromise must be negotiated based on the

premises that are accepted and agreed to by both parties.

Examples of published therapy materials:
1. *Developmental Learning Materials*
   Reaction Cards
   Alternative Cards
2. *Basic Thinking Skills*
   Critical Thinking Series
   Logic, Reasoning, and Arguments
3. *Manual of Exercises for Expressive Reasoning*
   Identifying Problems and Determining Solutions (pp. 143-147)
4. *Midwest Publications*
   Syllogisms, A1-C1

ASSOCIATED BEHAVIORS

Environmental management will often help to maximize the potential function of patients by avoiding or minimizing situations that would detract from performance. The stage of recovery and class of neurobehavioral disturbance will usually dictate the specific strategy. Techniques to deal with frequently occurring problem behaviors will be presented in the following section.

Confusion

Orientation of confused and disoriented patients to person, place, time, and illness can be accomplished in individual and group sessions. Orientation information should be reviewed with all patients as tolerated every morning and prior to each therapy session. Specific information reviewed (as tolerated by the patient) should include the patient's name, name of the facility, day, month, date, year, time, the names of each of the team members, and the time of each therapy appointment. The visual cues should be placed in each patient's room, to be utilized during orientation tasks; these include a calendar, a clock, a bulletin board, and a card on which the name of the hospital is printed. Pictures of each of the patient's clinicians, can also be placed on the bulletin board. A daily appointment schedule should be fastened to each patient's wheelchair indicating the time and type of each appointment. Initially, it might be helpful if someone, such as an aide or family members, stayed with the patient at all times.

Consistency is a must. Meal schedules, therapy schedules, visits by or to clinicians, and so forth must be kept constant. Routines must be established, and changes should be avoided until the confusion lessens. Order should be maintained in the patient's room (e.g., all items should be placed in a designated place and clutter should be minimized). All persons interacting with the patient should explain the purpose of each activity at the patient's level of comprehension. Redirect the patient to concrete tasks when necessary.

Quite often, return to a familiar environment, such as the patient's home, with family members will reduce confusion.

A reality orientation group is important at this point in treatment. Group activities should include a review of orientation information presented in individual sessions; familiarization with the physical plant in the patient's area of the hospital; a review of each group member's biographical information, including name, age, birth date, hometown, marital status, state, amount of education, and job; daily routines, including meals, therapies, and similar activities. The group activities improve orientation, increase selective attention, and provide opportunities for social interaction. The consistency of the group and the continual review of information concerning each member helps to orient each patient to others in his or her environment.

Orientation procedures vary as the patient's awareness increases and confusion decreases. Initially, the clinician must present all orientation information. Next, the clinician provides cues and encourages the patient to take more responsibility (e.g., the patient is to attend therapy appointments using a schedule card provided by the clinician). Finally, the patient should be required to function independently, such as to make a daily schedule, get to therapy appointments on time, request medication at appropriate time, and so forth.

Perseveration

When dealing with patients who have difficulty shifting their focus of attention, resulting in perseveration, care must be taken to pace interactions with the patient to allow disengagement from a stimulus before proceeding to the next task. Complexity and speed will often promote perseveration. Therefore, structure and slow pacing become critical. Providing pauses and then redirecting the patient's attention to another activity or sequence in an activity is often helpful.

Impulsivity or Distractibility

At times patients are unable to inhibit an inappropiate shifting of the focus of attention, resulting in distractibility. During these times, patients have a great deal of difficulty inhibiting impulses, and they do not monitor their behavior. Quite often these are premorbid behaviors that were amplified by the brain damage.

When distractibility occurs, treatment should be provided in a quiet setting with minimal or highly structured, controlled stimulation.

To treat impulsivity, a delay can be imposed before and after each of the patient's responses. Delays should also be used to deal with interfering needs, such as cigarette smoking, eating, or drinking.

Agitation

Agitation and outburst are common and to be expected problems as individuals recover. It is usually helpful to analyze the circumstances surrounding the agitation. Often the outburst can be seen as disinhibited, impulsive responses to environmental stimuli. Most people encounter situations in their daily activities that can provoke annoyance yet they usually inhibit the impulse to strike out. In the confusional state, the patient may be provoked by minor stimuli, such as being asked to perform a task that requires effort. The result might be an impulsive, disinhibited response to strike at the nearest clinician. The offending stimuli may be external and obvious or internal and not so obvious. This problem is often exacerbated by the distress associated with the inability to handle all the stimuli provided by the environment. The logical step here is simplify the structures of information presented to the patient and to minimize the environmental stimuli. Therapy may best be accomplished in a quiet room. It is often necessary to provide the patient with a private room and to minimize the number of people present at any given time. The elimination of offensive stimuli may be desirable but often difficult. Treatment sessions must be flexible. When patients become agitated, it is often best to change or discontinue specific tasks and to redirect their attention toward other tasks. Restraining, confronting, or placing demands on a patient often increases agitation. Attempts should be made to use tasks and stimuli that tend to decrease agitation, such as less demanding, gross motor activities, which also help to decrease the high energy level usually exhibited by agitated patients. Agitated patients should be placed in safe aras and can be encouraged to perform physical activities, such as punching a ball, throwing bean bags, and so forth.

A method of dealing with a specific agitated patient is provided in the following example.

A 17 year old boy with a posterior cerebral artery occlusion and an amnesic disorder was also noted to have outbursts of agitation. Impulsivity and disinhibition, however, were not significant features of his behavioral problems. The problem was analyzed more closely by the staff and it appeared that the outbursts occurred as part of the frustration of coping with his memory problem. When the nurse greeted him in the morning and asked him if he recalled his name or knew the date, he became embarrassed, frustrated, and agitated. Thereafter, the nurse greeted him by saying, "Good morning, this is Cathy. Today is Tuesday. Isn't it a nice day?". The other clinicians engaged in a similar strategy and the reports of agitated behavior ceased.

Denial of Deficits

Patients with high level deficits must recognize their deficits before motivation can improve. When patients are able, it is important to include them in goal setting. Usually the most successful work will be on areas suggested or agreed to by the patient. A useful technique is to list therapy goals reached jointly by the patient and clinician on the wall in the patient's room. Progress toward the goals should be charted daily in a place where the patient can witness and refer to the charts.

Group therapy is particularly helpful with this problem. Peer review and videotapings often increase awareness.

Psychiatric Disturbances and Substance Abuse

Psychiatric problems and alcohol or drug abuse that occur following closed head injury usually existed prior to the injury as well. The problems are often amplified following the injury. When these disturbances are present, rehabilitation prognosis is poor if they are not treated effectively. Unfortunately, participation in either psychiatric or substance abuse programs requires at least a cognitive level of functioning that permits simple problem solving and reasoning. When this level of processing is reached, the rehabilitation program should be postponed until the psychiatric, alcohol, or drug problems are controlled, or the programs should be provided simultaneously.

USE OF COMPUTERS DURING COGNITIVE REHABILITATION

For several reasons, computers can be helpful during the treatment of cognitive dysfunctions, such as attention, reaction time, memory, hand-eye coordination, language, perception, discrimination, and visual tacking (Bracy, 1983; Schmidt and Lynch, 1983).

1. A single stimulus can be presented in a highly controlled manner.

2. The patient is required to compete only with himself or

herself, and a sense of control over therapy and progress often results, which in turn leads to increased motivation and feelings of self-worth.

3. Accurate, objective, and immediate feedback is received.

4. Patients tend to enjoy using computers.

All computer training should be selected and monitored by certified clinicians as part of a comprehensive treatment program for each patient. Computers should never be used as a substitute for the clinician.

Most appropriate programs have been written for the Apple II Plus Computer. The Cognitive Rehabilitation publication (6555 Carrollton Avenue, Indianapolis, IN 46220) routinely lists new programs for head injured clients. When selecting computer programs, the clinician should consider the following (Wilson, 1983):

1. Consistent, controlled levels of difficulty within a task.

2. Lesson or file generating capability.

3. Concise, easy to follow instructions.

4. Consistent response format.

5. Accurate and age appropriate content.

6. Degree of supervision required.

7. Friendly, unambiguous, and informative feedback.

8. Control of variables or parameters (i.e., length of time the stimulus is displayed, length of response delay time, task speed, number of trials per set, level of difficulty, type of prompts, size of stimuli, schedule, timing, and type of reinforcement).

9. Method of keeping and reporting data.

GROUP THERAPY

In addition to individual therapy, group treatment should be provided. Group therapy gives patients opportunities to (1) increase social interaction and self-monitoring skills in a more natural communication environment; (2) increase self-esteem and self-motivation; (3) increase the ability to develop short- and long-term goals that are meaningful; (4) share feelings and needs; and (5) provide and receive peer review of behaviors.

Ben-Yishay (1979) emphasized the importance of providing the patient with a social group with which he or she can identify and belong. Feelings of safety and acceptance with the group were suggested as important.

The interdisciplinary approach to group treatment is most beneficial when there is participation by two or more disciplines in each group, including speech-language pathology, neuropsychology, occupational therapy, and so forth. Group leadership can be rotated. Tasks can be devised that accomplish different goals in the various disciplines—for example, the speech-language pathologist may emphasize appropriate organization of thoughts during the verbal presentation of an idea, whereas, the occupatonal therapist might emphasize the correct sequencing of items alone, as correct sequencing is necessary for all functional activities. Multiple group leadership also provides for appropriate modeling of social behaviors and cognitive strategies for the group members. However, group feedback, peer pressure, and observations made by the group members, rather than by the clinician leaders, should be stressed. Each group member must be given the responsibility to increase insight in addition to providing rewards and support for all other group members.

Groups function best with one clinician for every two to three clients. Groups should include patients functioning at similar levels. When patients' levels are too diverse, leaders need to provide significantly more structure and cueing, taking away from the natural group process.

Several types of groups will be reviewed. Specific suggestions include the following: (1) the cognitive level expected for group assignment; (2) the purpose or goals of the group; (3) specific therapy tasks to be introduced; and (4) suggested group leaders.

Low Level Group

Various names have been used by institutions for this type of group, including stimulation group, alerting group, attention group, and reality orientation group. A low level group is appropriate for patients for whom the major goal is to increase the ability to sustain attention to a variety of stimuli for specified periods of time. Patients at the discrimination level or the low organization level described earlier in this textbook are usually appropriate for a low level group. Usually, patients at lower levels are not yet attending well enough to benefit from role modeling or limit setting in a group environment. Furthermore, too much structure and individual attention needs to be provided for clients functioning at these lower cognitive levels, thus defeating the purpose of group interaction.

Behaviors that must be controlled in a low level group include perseveration, distractibility, and impulsivity. The major goals in this group include (1) increasing the ability to sustain attention to a particular task and to switch attention appropriately; and (2) increasing the ability to attend, organize, and put information into storage for appropriate retrieval. Leaders should be aware that patients at this level may not be consciously aware of cognitive rules (e.g., the patient may be able to choose the dissimilar block in an array of six, but may be unable to verbalize the reason for the choice).

In addition to the activities described in the sections on discrimination and organization presented earlier, additional tasks should focus on (1) increasing the ability to retain orientation information; (2) increasing the ability to follow more complex directions and simple conversation; and (3) increasing the ability to attend to a variety of stimuli.

This group can be organized by any discipline, as all disciplines tend to have similar goals with patients who function at this level. The group must be highly structured, and a significant amount of cueing must be provided by the clinicians. Minimal to moderate carryover from day to day should be expected from the patients.

Moderate Level Group

Two types of groups can be offered at this level. Groups include patients with organizational and problem-solving difficulties. Two different approaches to group rehabilitation of patients at this level can be stressed, including improving organization, retention, and problem-solving skills in functional tasks and increasing cognitive skills through movement from a concrete to a more abstract level in clinical tasks.

The major purpose of one group can be to aid clients in transferring learned organizational skills to functional tasks, such as planning a picnic. Specific activities include the following:

1. Thinking through and verbalizing a plan or general outline for the activity.

2. Detailing the steps necessary for each section of the activity (e.g., determining the number of people attending, planning the menu, contacting the cafeteria, and writing directions to the site).

It is obvious that each detail of the picnic would require a significant amount of attention, retention, organization, and problem solving.

Various modules or types of activities can be presented for this group, including the following: (1) Giving and following directions; (2) Emergency skills; (3) Skills around the house; (4) Shopping skills.

Each module can then be broken into smaller units. For example, the Giving and Following Directions module might consist of the following:

a. Following three-step verbal directions.

b. Giving verbal directions to a particular location.

c. Following written directions in filling out a form.
d. Following a written recipe.
e. Following test directions or game directions.
f. Giving or following map directions.

Leaders for this group can vary, but a combination of approaches by therapeutic recreation specialists, speech-language pathologists, occupational therapists, and physical therapists can be most beneficial. Leadership can be rotated, depending on the modules being stressed.

In this group, peer interaction is extremely important. Inappropriate behaviors, such as interrupting or swearing, are common and must be dealt with. A high degree of structure and cueing may still be necessary at this level.

The second type of group at the moderate level is one that is not functionally oriented but that attempts to move the patient to a more abstract level of functioning. This is carried out by increasing insight and decreasing the concreteness of responses. Given a problem, the patient is required to analyze the situation, generate possible solutions, apply a solution, and determine whether or not it solves the problem. Other group members evaluate the choices and decisions made. Numerous skills are involved in this process, including attention, discrimination, organization, and the various thought processes outlined earlier in this chapter. Several published materials offer stimuli for this level of group including the Mind Benders Series and Syllogisms (*Midwest Publications*). Other tasks might include the following:

1. Given one long word (e.g., notwithstanding), the patients are required to generate as many small words from it as possible.

2. Given two nonsense figures, the clients are to discuss their attributes to determine whether another nonsense figure might fit into the same category.

Group members must come up with correct solutions, and should also be required to verbalize all the steps taken in generating that solution. The application of the same strategy to other problems or situations can also be demonstrated.

An example of an appropriate activity is as follows. Given Figure 9-1, patients are asked to generate a response for the correct number of squares and rectangles in the picture. Working at a concrete level, a patient might quickly move through the picture counting up obvious squares and rectangles such as the large rectangle and smaller squares. A patient at a slightly higher level might apply some type of strategy, such as moving from left to right while counting up the squares and rectangles. Another patient might

Figure 9-1.

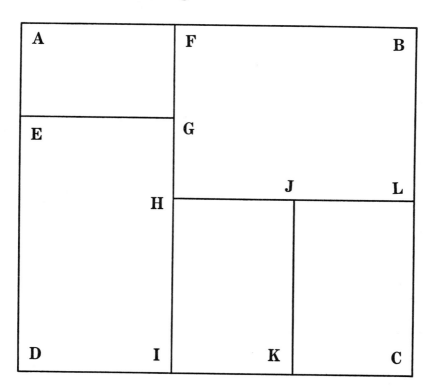

move from left to right using the letters to keep track as well as writing down each square or rectangle as he or she counts them. At the end of the allotted time, patients would then be required to give their responses and to explain how their responses were determined. Peer review and interaction are extremely important in working through problems such as this one. This group can probably be best organized by a neuropsychologist and a speech-language pathologist.

High Level Groups

Patients should be at the higher thought processing stage in the hierarchy presented earlier. This group is often provided on an out-patient therapy basis. The types of groups conducted at this level might include a higher level functional living skills group or community reentry group, a high level cognitive language group, a pragmatics group, and a social skills training group.

Functional Living Skills Group. Tasks in the functional living skills group would be geared toward community activities. Significantly less structure would be supplied by the leaders, and the group members would be responsible for conducting the majority of the sessions. A written contract might also be used at this level, obligating the patient to come to a certain number of sessions, behave in a certain manner, and so forth. Modules for the functional living skills group or the community reentry group would include the following:

1. Use of public transportation.
2. Finding a job.
3. Shopping skills.
4. Appropriate use of leisure time.

Again, each module could be broken down into many individual units, such as the following for "Finding a job":

1. Researching opportunities (this would involve the skills of knowing how to use a newspaper).
2. Filling out an application.
3. Interviewing.

Cognitive Language Group. The cognitive language group at this higher level would concentrate on the following:

1. Increasing speed and accuracy of problem solving.
2. Continuing to increase verbal organization and problem solving skills.
3. Increasing the ability to formulate and verbalize opinions.

Pragmatic Group. Patients functioning at this level may continue to demonstrate inappropriate communication-interaction skills as well as inappropriate social behaviors. A pragmatics group may improve the patients' abilities to appropriately employ pragmatic behaviors in a communication situation. The use of a videotape recording for this group is extremely important so that patients can actually watch their interactions for lack of facial expressions, lack of gestures, interrupting behaviors, and so forth. Group feedback should also be stressed. Additional behaviors or activities that might be included are the following:

1. Organization of thoughts before presenting an idea.
2. Verbally presenting ideas in an organized manner.
3. Responding appropriately to feedback.
4. Changing the subject appropriately.
5. Initiating a conversation with a friend or stranger.
6. Maintaining appropriate posture, eye contact, rate, social

distance, gestures, and intonation.

7. Employing appropriate turn-taking skills.

8. Controlling egocentric behaviors.

This group can be conducted by speech-language pathologists, psychologists, or occupational therapists.

Social Skills Training Group. Social competence is defined as the ability to interact appropriately with others and to interpret the behaviors of others accurately. Three skills basic to social competence are role taking, person perception, and perspective taking. Role taking is the ability to understand the social position of others. Person perception is the way we perceive others. Perspective taking is the ability to imagine physical manipulation. These skills can be analyzed into four sequentially dependent components. These are selective attention, response generation, response execution, and the appropriate response to feedback (Parrill-Burnstein, 1981).

A socialization group would break down various social skills and retrain the patients by increasing their insight into these situations. Examples of situations which might be included are (1) how to act appropriately at a party; or (2) how to act in a job interview. This group can be organized by psychologists, social service personnel, vocational rehabilitation counselors, or speech-language pathologists.

Sources:
Therapy Materials

American Guidance Services, Inc., Circle Pines, MN 55041.

Auditory Memory Training Exercises, The Alexander Graham Bell Association for the Deaf, 3417 Volta Place NW, Washington, DC 20007.

Basic Thinking Skills, Midwest Publication Co., PO Box 448, Pacific Grove, CA 93980.

Brain Link Software, 317 Montgomery, Ann Arbor, MI 48103.

Brubaker Workbook for Aphasia, Wayne State University Press, Detroit, MI 48202.

Compu-tations, Inc., PO Box 502, Troy, MI 48009.

Computer-Advanced Ideas, Inc., 1442 A, Walnut Street, Suite 341, Berkeley, CA 94709.

Davidson and Associates, 6069 Grove Oak Place, #12, Rancho Palos Verdes, CA 90274.

Developmental Learning Materials, One DLM Park, Allen, TX 75002.

Educational Activities, Inc., PO Box 392, Freeport, NY 11520.

Edu-Ware Services, Inc., 22222 Sherman Way, Canoga Park, CA 91303.

Hartley Courseware, PO Box 431, Dimondale, MI 48821.

Illinois Test of Psycholinguistic Abilities, Western Psychological Services, Publishers and Distributors, 12031 Wilshire Boulevard, Los Angeles, CA 90025.

Language Remediation and Expansion, Communication Skill Builders, 3130 North Dodge Boulevard, PO Box 42050, Tucson, AZ 85733.

Laureate Learning Systems, Mill Street, Burlington, VT 05401.

Life Science Associates, 1 Fenimore Road, Bayport, NY 11705.

Manual of Exercises for Expressive Reasoning, Lingui Systems, Inc., Suite 806, 1630 Fifth Avenue, Moline, IL 61265.

Midwest Publications, PO Box 448, Pacific Grove, CA 93950.

Minnesota Educational Computing Consortium, 2520 Broadway Drive, St. Paul, MN 55113.

Modern Education Corporation, PO Box 721, Tulsa, OK 74101.

Program Design, Inc., 11 Idar Street, Greenwich, CT 06830.

Psychological Software Services, PO Box 29205, Indianapolis, IN 46229.

Reader's Digest Skill Builders, Pleasantville, NY 10570.

Slosson Educational Publications, Inc., PO Box 280, East Aurora, NY 14052.

Speech and Language Rehabilitation: A Workbook for the Neurologically Impaired and Language Delayed, Vol. I., R. L. Keith. Interstate Printers and Publishers, Inc., Danville, IL 61832.

Sunset Software, 11750 Sunset Boulevard, Suite 414, Los Angeles, CA 90049.

Teachers College Press, 81 Adams Drive, Totawa, NJ 07502.

Teaching Resources, Fokes Sentence Builder, 50 Pond Street, Hingham, MA 02043.

The Amazing Adventures of Harvey Crumbaker Skills for Living, Lakeshore Curriculum Materials Co., 2695 E Dominguez St, PO Box 6261, Carson, CA 90749.

Therapy Guide for the Adult with Language and Speech Disorders, Vol. I, Visiting Nurse Service, Inc., 1200 McArthur Drive, Akron, OH 44320.

Therapy Guide for the Adult with Language and Speech Disorders, Vol. II, Visiting Nurse Service, Inc., 1200 McArthur Drive, Akron, OH 44320.

The Thinking Skills Workbook: A Cognitive Skills Remediation Manual for Adults, by L. Carter, J. Caruso, M. Languirand, and M.A. Berard. Charles C Thomas, Publisher, 2600 S First St, Springfield, IL 62717.

University Park Press, 300 North Charles Street, Baltimore, MD 21201.

References

Adamovich, B.B. A comparison of the processes of memory and perception between aphasic and non-brain injured adults. *Clinical Aphasiology Conference Proceedings,* Minneapolis, BRK Publishers, 1978.

Adamovich, B.B. Language versus cognition: The speech-language pathologist's role. *Clinical Aphasiology Conference Proceedings,* Kerrville, TX. Minneapolis, BRK Publishers, 1981, pp. 277-280.

Adamovich, B.B., and Brooks, R. A diagnostic protocol to assess the communication deficits of patients with right hemisphere damage. In R.H. Brookshire (Ed.), *Clinical Aphasiology Conference Proceedings,* Kerrville, TX. Minneapolis, BRK Publishers, 1981, pp. 244-253.

Adamovich, B.B., and Henderson, J.A. Cognitive deficits post traumatic head injury: Diagnostic and treatment implications. Paper presented at ASHA Annual Convention, Cincinnati, November, 1983.

Adamovich, B.B., and Henderson, J.A. Can we learn more from word fluency measures with aphasic, right brain injured, and closed head trauma patients? *Clinical Aphasiology Conference Proceedings,* Seabrook Island, South Carolina, 1984.

Adamovich, B.B., and Henderson, J.A. An investigation of the cognitive changes of head trauma patients following a treatment period. Paper presented at ASHA Convention, Toronto, 1982.

Adams, J.H., Graham, D.I., and Gennarelli, T.A. Acceleration induced head injury in the monkey. *Acta Neuropathologica,* 7:26-28, 1981.

Adams, J.H., Graham, D.I., Murray, L.S., and Scott, G. Diffuse axonal injury due to nonmissile head injury in humans: An analysis of 45 cases. *Annals of Neurology, 12:*557-563, 1982.

Adams, J.H., Scott, J.F., Parker, L.S., Graham, D.I., and Doyle, D. The contusion index: A quantitative approach to cerebral contusions in head injury. *Applied Neuropathology, 63:*319-324, 1980.

Adams, R., and Victor, M. *Principles of Neurology.* New York, McGraw-Hill Book Company, 1977.

Alexander, M.L. Traumatic brain injury. In D.F. Benson and D. Blumer (Eds.), *Psychiatric Aspects of Neurological Disease,* Volume II. New York, Grune & Stratton, 1982.

Anderson, D.W., and McLaurin, R.L. (Eds.). Report on national head and spinal cord injury conducted for NINCDS. *Journal of Neurosurgery,* Suppl., S1-S43, 1980.

Anderson, R.P., Halcomb, C.G., and Doyle, R.B. The measurement of attentional deficits. *Exceptional Children, 39:*534-539, 1973.

Annegers, J.F., and Kurland, L.T. The epidemeology of central nervous system trauma. In G.L. Odom (Ed.), *Central Nervous System Trauma Research Status Report.* Report prepared for NINCDS, NIH, Public Health Service, 1979.

Annett, M. The classification of instances of four common class concepts by children and adults. *British Journal of Educational Psychology, 29:*223-236, 1959.

Asch, S.E. Perceptual conditions of association. In M. Hendle (Ed.), *Documents of Gestalt Psychology.* Berkeley, University of California Press, 1961.

Astrom, K., Eecken, H., and Adams, R. Traumatic Diseases of the Brain. In Reeves (Ed.), *Disorders of the Nervous System.* Chicago, Year Book Medical Publishers, 1980.

Atkinson, R.C., and Shiffrin, R.M. Human memory: A proposed system and its control processes. In K.N. Spence, and J.N. Spence (Eds.), *The Psychology of Learning and Motivation: Advances in Research and Theory,* Vol. 2. New York, Academic Press, 1968.

Auerbach, S.H., Moore, S., and Weinberg, R. Neurobehavioral subtypes in closed head injury: The identification of medial limbic and basolateral limbic subtypes. Annual Conference on Cognitive Rehabilitation, Indianapolis, April 1 and 2, 1984.

Baddeley, A.D. *The Psychology of Memory.* New York, Basic Books, 1976.

Ballantine, H.T., Jr., Cassidy, W.L., Flanagan, N.B., and Marino, R. Stereotaxic anterior cingulotomy for neuropsychiatric illness and intractable pain. *Journal of Neurosurgery, 26:* 488-495, 1967.

Bates, E. Pragmatics and sociolinguistics in child language. In D.M. Morehead and A.E. Morehead (Eds.), *Normal and Deficient Child Language.* Baltimore, University Park Press, 1976.

Becker, L.D., Bender, N.N., and Morrison, G. Measuring Impulsivity – Reflection: A critical review. *Journal of Learning Disabilities, 11*(10):626-632, 1978.

Bellugi, U., and Studdert-Kennedy, M. Signed and spoken language: Biological constraints on linguistic form. Report of the Dahlem Workshop, Berlin, March 24-28, 1980.

Benson, D.F., and Blumer, D. Commentary to traumatic brain injury by M.L. Alexander. In D.F. Benson and D. Blumer (Eds.), *Psychiatric Aspects of Neurologic Disease,* Volume II. New York, Grune & Stratton, 1982.

Benton, A.L. Behavioral consequences of closed head injury. In G.L. Odom (Ed.), *Central Nervous System Trauma Research Status Report.* Report printed with and from NINCDS, NIH, Public Health Service, 1979, pp. 220-231.

Ben-Yishay, Y. Working approaches to remediation of cognitive deficits in brain damaged patients. Institute of Rehabilitation Medicine, New York University Medical Center, Department of Behavioral Sciences, Supplements for June 1978; May 1979; May 1980 (studies for grant 12 P-556 23 and RT-93).

Berlin, H. *Studies in the Cognitive Basis of Language Development.* New York, Academic Press, 1975.

Bever, T.G. Cerebral asymmetrics in humans are due to the differentiation of two incompatible processes: Holistic and analytic. *Annals of the New York Academy of Sciences, 265*:252-262, 1975.

Bloom, L. *Language Development: Form and Function in Emerging Grammars.* Cambridge, MA: MIT Press, 1970.

Blumer, D., and Benson, D.F. Personality changes with frontal and temporal lobe lesions. In D.F. Benson and D. Blumer (Eds.), *Psychiatric Aspects of Neurologic Disease.* New York, Grune & Stratton, 1975.

Bower, G. H. Contacts of cognitive psychology with social learning theory. *Cognitive Therapy and Research, 2*(2):123-146, 1978.

Bracy, O. Computer based cognitive rehabilitation *Cognitive Rehabilitation, 1*(1): 7-8, 1983.

Brierly, J.D. Neuropathy of amnestic states. In C.W.M. Whitty and O.L. Zangwill (Eds.), *Amnesia*. Boston, Buttersworth, 1977.

Broadbent, D.E. *Perception and communication*. London, Pergamon Press, 1958.

Brooks, D.N. Recognition memory and head injury. *Journal of Neurology, Neurosurgery, and Psychiatry, 37:*794-801, 1974.

Brooks, D.N., and Aughton, M.E. Cognitive recovery during the first year after severe blunt head injury. Head Injuries Symposium, 1976, pp. 166-171. Department of Psychological Medicine, University of Glasgow, Scotland.

Brooks, D.N., Aughton, M.E., Bond, M.R., Jones, P., and Rizvi, S. Cognitive sequelae in relationship to early indices of severity of brain damage after severe blunt head injury. *Journal of Neurology, Neurosurgery, and Psychiatry, 43:*529-534, 1980.

Brown, M.H., and Lighthill, J.A. Selective anterior cingulotomy: A psychosurgical evaluation. *Journal of Neurosurgery, 29:*513-519, 1968.

Bruner, J.S. The course of cognitive growth. *American Psychologist, 19:*1-15, 1964.

Bruner, J.S. *Beyond the Information Given*. New York: W.W. Norton, 1973.

Bruner, J.S. From communication to language. A psychological perspective. *Cognition, 3:*255-287, 1975.

Bruner, J.S., Goodnow, J.J., and Austin, G.A. *A Study of Thinking*. New York: John Wiley, 1956.

Bruner, J.S., Oliver, R., and Greenfield, P. (Eds.). *Studies in Cognitive Growth*. New York, Wiley Press, 1966.

Bryan, T. The effects of forced mediation upon short-term memory of children with learning disabilities. *Journal of Learning Disabilities, 5:*605-606, 1972.

Bryden, M.P., and Rainey, C. Left-right differences in tachistocopic recognition. *Journal of Experimental Psychology, 66:*568-571, 1963.

Buschbaum, M., and Fedio, P. Hemispheric difference in evoked potentials to verbal and nonverbal stimuli on the left and right visual fields. *Physiology and Behavior, 5:*207-210, 1970.

Case, R. Structures and strictures: Some functional limitations on the course of cognitive growth. *Cognitive Psychology, 6*:544-573, 1974.

Case, R. Intellectual development from birth to adulthood: A neo-piagetian interpretation. In R. Sieglar (Ed.), *Children's Thinking: What Develops?* Hillsdale, NJ: Lawrence Erlbaum Associates, 1978.

Clark, E. What's in a word? On the child's acquisition of semantics in his first language. In T. Moore (Ed.), *Cognitive Development and the Acquisition of Language.* New York, Academic Press, 1973a, pp. 65-70.

Clark, H.H. Space, time semantics, and the child. In T. Moore (Ed.), *Cognitive Development and Acquisition of Language.* New York, Academic Press, 1973b, 27-63.

Clifton, G.L., Grossman, R.G., Makala, M.E., Miner, M.E., Handel, S., and Sadhu, V. Neurological course and computerized tomography findings after severe closed head injury. *Journal of Neurological Surgery, 52*:611-624, 1980.

Committee to Study Head Injury Nomenclature Report. *Clinical Neurosurgical Journal, 12*:386-387, 1966.

Conkey, R.C. Psychological changes associated with head injuries. *Archives of Psychology, 33*:232, 1938.

Cope, N., and Hall, K. Head injury rehabilitation: Benefit of early intervention. *Archives of Physical Medicine and Rehabilitation, 63*:433-437, 1982.

Courville, C.B. *Commotia Cerebri.* Los Angeles, San Lucas Press, 1953.

Craik, F.I.M., and Lockhart, R.S. Levels of processing: A framework for memory research. *Journal of Verbal Learning and Verbal Behavior, 11*:671-684, 1972.

Cruickshank, W.M. (Ed.). *The Teacher of Brain-Injured Children.* Syracuse, NY, Syracuse University Press, 1966.

Davies, P. *The American Heritage Dictionary of the English Language.* New York, Houghton Mifflin, 1982.

Denny-Brown, D., and Russell, W.R. Experimental cerebral concussion. *Brain, 64*:93-164, 1941.

Douglas, V.I. Stop, look and listen: The problem of sustained attention and impulse control in hyperactive and normal children. *Canadian Journal of Behavioral Science, 4:*259-281, 1972.

Doyle, R.B., Anderson, R.P., and Halcomb, C.G. Attentional deficits and the effects of visual distractions. *Journal of Learning Disabilities, 9*(1):48-54, 1976.

Drachman, D.A., and Leavitt, J. Human memory and the cholinergic system. *Archives of Neurology, 30:*113-121, 1974.

Dykman, R.A., Ackerman, P.T., and Clements, S.D. Specific learning disabilities: An attentional deficit syndrome. In H.R. Myklebust (Ed.), *Progress in Learning Disabilities,* Vol. II. New York, Grune & Stratton, 1971.

Egeland, B. Training impulsive children in the use of more efficient scanning techniques. *Child Development, 45:*165-171, 1974.

Eimas, P.D. A developmental study of hypothesis behavior and focusing. *Journal of Experimental Child Psychology, 8:*160-172, 1969.

Eimas, P.D. Effects of memory aids on hypothesis behavior and focusing in young children and adults. *Journal of Experimental Psychology, 10:*319-336, 1970.

Feeney, D.M., Gonzalez, A., and Law, W.A. Amphetamine, haloperidol and experience interact to affect rate of recovery after motor cortex injury. *Science, 217:*855-857, 1982.

Fields, J.H. *A Study of the Epidemiology of Head Injury in England and Wales.* London, Department of Health and Social Security, 1976.

Finch, A.J., and Spirito, A. Use of cognitive training to change cognitive processes. *Exceptional Education Quarterly, 1*(1):31-39, 1980.

Flavell, J.H. Developmental studies of mediated memory. In H.W. Reese and L.P. Lipsitt (Eds.), *Advances in Child Development and Behavior* (Vol. 5). New York, Academic Press, 1970.

Flavell, J.H., and Wellman, H.M. Metamemory. In R.V. Kail and J.W. Hagen (Eds.), *Memory in Cognitive Development.* Hillsdale, NJ, Lawrence Erlbaum Associates, 1977.

Fodor, I.E. Impairment of memory functions after acute head injury. *Journal of Neurology, Neurosurgery, and Psychiatry, 35*(6):818-824, 1972.

Foltz, E.L. Cingular Lesions: Current status and use of rostral cingulotomy. *Southern Medical Journal, 61*:899, 1968.

Fuster, J.M. *The Prefrontal Cortex. Anatomy, Physiology and Neuropsychology.* New York, Raven Press, 1980.

Gagne, R.M., and Briggs, L.J. *Principles of Instructional Design.* New York, Holt, Rinehart, Winston, 1979.

Galin, D. Implications for psychiatry of left and right cerebral specialization. *Archives of General Psychology, 1*:572-583, 1974.

Galin, D., and Ornstein, R. Lateral specialization of cognitive mode: An EEG study. *Psychophysiology, 9*:412-418, 1972.

Gazzaniga, M.S. The frontal lobes. *Handbook of Behavioral Neurobiology: Neuropsychology* (Vol. 2). New York, Plenum Press, 1979.

Gazzaniga, M.S., and Hillyard, S.A. Language and speech capacity of the right hemisphere. *Neuropsychologia, 9*:273-280, 1971.

Gazzaniga, M.S., and Sperry, R.W. Language after section of the cerebral commissures. *Brain, 90*:131-138, 1967.

Gennarelli, T.A., Adams, J.H., and Graham, D.J. Acceleration induced head injury in the monkey. II. The model, its mechanical and physiological correlates. *Acta Neuropathologica* (Berlin), Suppl. *7*:23-25, 1981.

Gennarelli, T.A., Thibault, L.E., Adams, J.H., Graham, D.I., Thompson, C.J., and Marcincin, R.P. Diffuse axonal injury and traumatic coma in the primate. *Annals of Neurology, 12*:564-574, 1982.

Geschwind, H. Disorders of attention: A frontier in neuropsychology. *Philosophical Transactions of the Royal Society of London, 298*:173-185, 1982.

Gholson, B., Levine, M., and Phillips, S. Hypothesis strategies and stereotypes in discrimination learning. *Journal of Experimental Child Psychology, 13*:423-446, 1972.

Gholson, B., and McConville, K. Effects of stimulus differentiation training upon hypothesis, strategies and stereotypes in discrimination learning among kindergarten children. *Journal of Experimental Child Psychology, 18*:81-97, 1974.

Gibson, E.J. Principles of perceptual learning and development. New York, Appleton, 1969.

Goldberg, E., Gratzman, L.J., Mattis, S., Hughes, J.E.O., Bilder, R.M., and Sirio, C.A. Effects of cholinergic treatment on post traumatic anterograde amnesia. *Archives of Neurology,* 39, 1982.

Goodglass, H., and Kaplan, E. *The Assessment of Aphasia and Related Disorders.* Philadelphia, Lea and Febiger, 1972.

Goodglass, H., and Kaplan, E. The assessment of cognitive deficits in the brain injured patient. In M.S. Gazzaniga (Ed.), *Handbook of Behavioral Neurobiology Neuropsychology.* New York, Plenum Press, 1979, pp. 3-22.

Graham, D.I., Adams, H., and Doyle, D. Ischemic brain damage in fatal nonmissile head injuries. *Journal of Neurological Sciences, 39:*213-234, 1978.

Groat, R.A., and Simmons, J.Q. The loss of nerve cells in experimental cerebral concussion. *Journal of Neuropathology and Experimental Neurology, 9:*150, 1950.

Groher, M. Language and memory disorders following closed head trauma. *Journal of Speech and Hearing Research, 20:*212-223, 1977.

Gronwall, D. Placed auditory serial addition task: A measure of recovery from concussion. *Perceptual Motor Skills, 44:*367-373, 1977.

Gruzzman, M. Reversal operation after brain damage. *Brain and Cognition, 1:*331-354, 1982.

Hagen, C., and Malkmus, D. Intervention strategies for language disorders secondary to head trauma. American Speech-Language-Hearing Association Convention, Short Course, Atlanta, 1979.

Halford, G. Toward a redefinition of cognitive developmental states. In J.R. Kirby and J.B. Biggs (Eds.), *Cognition, Development and Instruction.* New York, Academic Press, 1980.

Hallahan, D.P., Kaufman, J.M., and Ball, D.W. Effects of stimulus attenuation on selective attention performance of children. *Journal of Genetic Psychology, 125:*71-77, 1974.

Heilman, K.M., Safran, A., and Geschwind, N. Closed head trauma and aphasia. *Journal of Neurology, Neurosurgery, and Psychiatry, 34:*265-269, 1971a.

Heilman, K.M., Watson, R.T., and Schulman, H.M. A unilateral memory defect. *Journal of Neurology, Neurosurgery, and Psychiatry, 37:*790-793, 1971b.

Heiskanen, O., and Sipponen, P. Prognosis of severe brain injury. *Acta Neurologica Scandinavica, 46:*343, 1970.

Helm, N.A., Butler, R.B., and Benson, D.F. Acquired stuttering. *Neurology, 27:*349, 1977.

Herman, J.F., and Seigel, H.W. The development of cognitive mapping of the large-scale environment. *Journal of Experimental Child Psychology, 26:*389-406, 1978.

Holburn, A.H.S. Mechanisms of head injuries. *Lancet, 2:*438-441, 1943.

Holland, A.L. When is aphasia aphasia? The problem of closed head injury. *Clinical Aphasiology Conference Proceedings,* University of Pittsburgh, Pennsylvania, 1982.

Jennett, B., and Bond, M. Assessment outcome after severe brain damage: Practical scale. *Lancet, 1:*480-484, 1975.

Jennett, B., Snoak, J., Bond, M., and Brooks, N. Disability after severe head injury: Observations on the use of the Glasgow Outcome Scale. *Journal of Neurology, Neurosurgery, and Psychiatry, 44:*285-293, 1981.

Johnson, D.J., and Mykelbust, H. *Learning Disabilities: Educational Principles and Practices.* New York, Grune & Stratton, 1967.

Kalsbeek, W.D., McLaurin, R.L., Harris, B.S.H., and Miller, J. The national head and spinal cord injury survey: Major findings. In D.W. Anderson and R.L. McLaurin (Eds.), *Report on the National Head and Spinal Cord Injury Survey* (Special Supplement). *Journal of Neurosurgery, 53:*513-531, 1980.

Keogh, B.K. Hyperactivity and learning disorders: Review and speculation. *Exceptional Children, 38:*101-110, 1971.

Keogh, B.K., and Margolis, J. Learn to labor and wait: Attentional problems of children with learning disorders. *Journal of Learning Disabilities, 9*(5):276-286, 1976.

Kimura, D. Some effects of temporal lobe damage on auditory perception. *Canadian Journal of Psychology, 23:*445-458, 1961.

Kinsbourne, M. Eye and head turning indicates cerebral lateralization. *Science, 176:*539-541, 1972.

Kirby, J.R. Individual differences and cognitive processes: Instructional application and methodological difficulties. In J.R. Kirby and J.B. Biggs, *Cognition Development, and Instruction.* New York, Academic Press, 1980.

Kirby, J.R., and Biggs, J.B. *Cognition, Development, and Instruction.* New York, Academic Press, 1980.

Knight, G.C. Selective Tractotomy in the surgical treatment of mental illness. *Journal of Neurology, Neurosurgery, and Psychiatry, 28:*304, 1965.

Kohler, W. On the nature of associations. *Proceedings of the American Philosophical Society, 84:*489-502, 1941.

Kraus, J.F. Injury to the head and spinal cord: The epidemiological relevance of the medical literature published from 1960-1978. *Journal of Neurosurgery* (Suppl.), *53:*3-10, 1980.

Lawson, M.J. Metamemory: Making decisions about strategies. In J.R. Kirby and J.B. Biggs, *Cognition Development and Instruction.* New York, Academic Press, 1980.

LeBeau, J. The cingular and precingular areas in psychosurgery-agitated behavior, obsessive-compulsive states, epilepsy. *Arch. Psychiatrica Neurologica Scandinavica, 27:*304, 1952.

LeMay, M., and Geschwind, N. Asymmetries of the human cerebral hemispheres. In A. Carmazza and E. Zurif (Eds.), *Language Acquisition and Language Breakdown.* Baltimore, Johns Hopkins University Press, 1978.

Levin, H.S. Aphasia in closed head injury. In M.T. Sarno (Ed.), *Acquired Aphasia.* New York, Academic Press, 1981.

Levin, H.S., Benton, A.L., and Grossman, R.G. *Neurobehavioral Consequences of Closed Head Injury.* New York, Oxford University Press, 1982.

Levin, H.S., Grossman, R.G., and Kelly, P. Short-term recognition memory in relation to severity of head injury. *Cortex, 12:*175-185, 1976.

Levin, H.S., Grossman, R.G., Sarwar, M., and Meyers, C.A. Linguistic recovery after closed head injury. *Brain and Language, 12:*360-374, 1981.

Levin, H.S., O'Donnell, V.M., and Grossman, R.G. The Galveston orientation and amnesia test. *Journal of Nervous and Mental Disease, 167:*675-684, 1979.

Levy, J., Trevarthen, C., and Sperry, R.W. Perception of bilateral chimeric figures following hemispheric disconnection. *Brain, 95:*61-78, 1972.

Lezak, M. Recovery of memory and learning functions following traumatic brain injury. *Cortex, 15:*63-72, 1979.

Lipper, S., and Tuchman, M.D. Treatment of chronic post-traumatic organic brain syndrome with dextro-amphetamine: First reported case. *Journal of Nervous and Mental Disease, 162:*366-371, 1976.

Livingston, K.E., and Escobar, A. Tentative limbic system models for certain patterns of psychiatric disorders. In L.V. Laitinen and K.E. Livingston (Eds.), *Surgical Approaches in Psychiatry.* Baltimore, University Park Press, 1972.

Luria, A.R. The role of speech in the regulation of normal and abnormal behavior. New York, Liveright, 1961.

Mackay, D. Cognitive behavior therapy. *British Journal of Hospital Medicine,* 242-247, 1982..

Mahut, H., Zda-Morgan, S., and Moss, M. Hippocampal resections impair associative learning and recognition memory in the monkey. *Journal of Neuroscience, 2:*1214-1229, 1982.

Mandleberg, I.A. Cognitive recovery after severe head injury: WAISA verbal and performance IQ's as a function of post traumatic amnesia and time from injury. *Journal of Neurology, Neurosurgery, and Psychiatry, 29:*1001-1007, 1976.

Marshall, J.C., and Newcombe, F. The structuring of language by biological and neurological processes. Group report. In U. Bellugi and M. Studdert-Kennedy (Eds.), *Signed and Spoken Language: Biological Constraints on Linguistic Form.* Report on the Dahlem Workshop, Berlin, March 24-28, 1980.

Marshall, R.C. Language and speech recovery in a case of viral encephalitis. *Brain and Language, 17:*316-326, 1982.

Martin, R.C. and Caramazza, A. Short-term memory performance in the absence of phonological coding. *Brain and Cognition, 1:*50-70, 1982.

McNeil, M. The nature of aphasia in adults. In N.I. Lass, L. McReynolds, J. Northern, and D. Yoder (Eds.), *Speech, Language and Hearing.* Philadelphia, W.B. Saunders, 1981.

Meichenbaum, D. Cognitive behavior modification with exceptional children: A promise yet unfulfilled. *Exceptional Education Quarterly, 1*(1):83-88, 1980.

Milner, B. Laterality effects in audition. In V.B. Mountcastle (Ed.), *Interhemispheric Relations and Cerebral Dominance.* Baltimore, Johns Hopkins Press, 1962.

Milner, B. Brain mechanisms suggested by studies of temporal lobes. In F.L. Darley *Brain Mechanism Underlying Speech and Language.* New York, Grune & Stratton, 1967.

Milner, B. Residual intellectual memory deficits after head injury. In A.E. Walker, E.F. Caveness, and M. Crutchley (Eds.), *The Late Effects of Head Injury.* Springfield, IL, Charles C Thomas, 1968.

Milner, B. Interhemispheric differences and psychological process. *British Medical Bulletin, 27:*272-287, 1971.

Moore, R.Y. Catecholamine neuron systems in brain. *Annals of Neurology, 12:*321-327, 1982.

Muma, J.R. *Language Handbook: Concepts Assessment and Intervention.* Englewood Cliffs, N.J., Prentice-Hall, 1978.

Myers, R.E. Function of corpus callosum in interocular transfer. *Brain, 79:*358-363, 1956.

Nauta, W.H.J. Hippocampal projections and related neural pathways to the midbrain in the cat. *Brain, 81:*319, 1958.

Nauta, W.H.J. Neural associations of the amygdaloid complex in the monkey. *Brain, 85:*505-520, 1962.

Nauta, W.H.J. Some neural pathways related to the limbic system. In W.L. Ramsey and R.J. O'Doherty (Eds.), *Electrical Studies of the Unanesthetized Brain.* New York, Paul B. Hoeber, 1960.

Nebes, R.D. Hemispheric spatialization in commissurotomized man. *Psychological Bulletin, 81:*1-14, 1974.

Neilson, J.M. Correlation of sites of lesions with symptoms. *Journal of Nervous and Mental Disease, 118:*429, 1953.

Neisser, V. *Cognition and Reality: Principles and Implications of Cognitive Psychology.* San Francisco, W.H. Freeman, 1976.

Nelson, K. Structure and strategy in learning to talk. *Monographs of the Society for Research in Child Development, 38:*429, 1973.

Norman, D.A. Descriptions: An intermediate stage in memory retrieval. Cognitive Psychology, 11:107-123, 1979.

Norman, D.A. Toward a theory of memory and attention. *Psychological Review, 75*(6):522-536, 1968.

Notelting, R. Stages and mechanisms in the development of the concept of proportion in the child and adolescent. Paper presented at the 5th Interdisciplinary Seminar on Piagetian Theory and its Implications for the Helping Professions. Los Angeles, University of Southern California, 1975.

Offenbach, S.I. A developmental study of hypothesis testing and cue selection strategies. *Developmental Psychology, 10*(4): 484-490, 1974.

Ommaya, A.K., and Gennarelli, T.A. Cerebral concussion and traumatic unconsciousness. *Brain, 97*:633-654, 1974.

Oppenheimer, D.R. Microscopic lesions in the brain following head injury. *Journal of Neurology, Neurosurgery, and Psychiatry, 31*:299-306, 1968.

Papez, J.W. A proposed mechanism of emotion. *Archives of Neurology and Psychiatry, 38*:725, 1937.

Parrill-Burnstein, M. Teaching kindergarten children to solve problems: An information processing approach. *Child Development, 40*(3):700-706, 1978.

Parrill-Burnstein, M. *Problem Solving and Learning Disabilities: An Information Processing Approach.* New York, Grune & Stratton, 1981.

Parrill-Burnstein, M., and Baker-Ward, L. Learning Disabilities: A social cognitive difference. *Learning Disabilities: An Audio Journal for Continuing Education, 3*(10), 1979.

Patten, B.M. *Modality Specific Memory Disorders.* New York, Neurological Institute, 1982.

Penfield, W., and Roberts, L. *Speech and Brain Mechanisms.* Princeton, N.J., Princeton University Press, 1959.

Phillips, S., and Levine, M. Probing for hypotheses with adults and children: Blank trials and introtracts. *Journal of Experimental Psychology (General, 194*:327-354, 1975.

Piaget, J. *Play, Dreams and Imitation in Childhood.* New York, W.W. Norton, 1962.

Piaget, J. Le langage et les operations intellectuelles. In J. de Ajuriaquerra, F. Bresson, P. Fraisse, B. Inhelder, P. Oleron, and J. Piaget (Eds.), *Problemes de psycho-linguistique.* Paris, Presses Universitaires de France, 1963.

Piaget, J. *Psychology of Intelligence.* Tolowa, N.J., Littlefield, Adams, 1966.

Piaget, J. *The Child's Conception of the World.* Patterson, N.J., Littlefield, Adams, 1969.

Piaget, J., and Inhelder, B. *The Psychology of the Child.* New York, Basic Books, 1969.

Pick, A.D., Frankel, D.G., and Hess, V.L. Children's attention: The development of selectivity. In E.M. Hetherington (Ed.), *Review of Child Development Research* (Vol. 5). Chicago, University of Chicago Press, 1975.

Piller, L., and Gordon, W. Interventions for cognitive deficits in brain injured adults. *Journal of Consulting and Clinical Psychology, 49*(6):822-834, 1981.

Plum, F., Gjedde, A., and Samson, F.E. Neuroanatomical functional mapping by the radioactive 2-dioxy-d-glucose method. *Neurosciences Research Program Bulletin, 14:*457-518, 1976.

Powell, T.P.S. Sensory convergence in the cerebal cortex. In L.V. Laitinen and K.E. Livingston (Eds.), *Surgical Approaches in Psychiatry.* Baltimore; University Park Press, 1972.

Pudenz, R.H., and Sheldon, C.H. The lucite calvarium: A model for direct observation of the brain. *Journal of Neurosurgery, 3:*487-505, 1946.

Reichert, W.H., and Blass, J.P. A placebo controlled trial shows no effect of vasopression in recovery from closed head injury. *Annals of Neurology, 12:*390-392, 1982.

Risberg, J., Halsey, J.H., Wells, E.L., and Wilson, E.M. Hemispheric specialization in normal man studied by bilateral measurements of the regional cerebral blood flow: A study with the 133 Xe inhalation technique. *Brain, 98:*511-524, 1975.

Rosch, E.H. On the internal structure of perceptual and semantic categories. In T.E. Moore, III, *Cognitive Development and the Acquisition of Language.* New York, Academic Press, 1973, pp. 111-144.

Ross, A.Q. *Psychological Aspects of Learning Disabilities and Reading Disorders.* New York, McGraw-Hill Book Company, 1976.

Rusk, H.A., Block, J.M., and Lowman, E.W. Rehabilitation following traumatic brain damage: Immediate and long term follow-up results in 127 cases. *Medical Clinics of North America, 53:*677-684, 1969.

Sarno, M.T. The nature of verbal impairment after closed head injury. *Journal of Nervous and Mental Disease, 168:*685-692, 1980.

Schmidt, N., and Lynch, W. Ask the experts. *National Head Injury Foundation, Inc., Newsletter* (Volume III), No. 2, Winter, 1983.

Sekino, H., Nakamura, N., Satoh, J., Kikuchu, K., and Sanada, S. Brain lesions detected by CT scans in cases of minor head injuries. *Neurologia Medico-Chirurgica,* (Tokyo), *21:*677-683, 1981.

Shaw, R.E., and Cutting, J.E. Clues from an ecological theory of event perception. In U. Bellugi and M. Studdert-Kennedy (Eds.), *Signed and Spoken Language: Biological Constraints on Linguistic Form.* Report of the Dahlem Workshop, Berlin, March 24-28, 1980.

Smith, E. Influence of site of impact on cognitive impairment persisting long after severe closed head injury. *Journal of Neurology, Neurosurgery, and Psychiatry, 37:*319-726, 1974.

Springer, S.P., and Deutsch, G. *Left Brain, Right Brain.* San Francisco, W.H. Freeman, 1981.

Stevens, J.R., and Livemore, A. Kindling of the mesolimbic dopamine system: Animal model of psychosis. *Neurology, 28:*35-46, 1978.

Strich, S.J. Shearing of nerve fibres as a cause of brain damage due to head injury. *Lancet, 2:*443-448, 1961.

Stuss, D.T., and Benson, D.F. Frontal lobe lesions and behavior. In A. Kertesz (Ed.), *Localization in Neuropsychology.* New York, Academic Press, 1983, pp. 429-455.

Stuss, D.T., and Benson, D.F. Neuropsychological studies of the frontal lobes. *Psychological Bulletin, 95:*3-28, 1984.

Suiter, M.L., and Potter, R.E. The effects of paradigmatic organization on verbal recall. *Journal of Learning Disabilities, 11*(4):247-250, 1978.

Swanson, H.L. Nonverbal visual short-term memory as a function of age and dimensionality in learning-disabled children. *Child Development, 48:*51-55, 1977a.

Swanson, H.L. Response strategies and stimulus salience with learning disabled and mentally retarded children on a short-term memory task. *Journal of Learning Disabilities,* *10*(10):635-642, 1977b.

Thomsen, I.V. Evaluation and outcome of traumatic aphasia in patients with severe verified focal lesions. *Folia Phoniatrica,* *28:*362-377, 1976.

Torgensen, J.K. Factors related to poor performance on memory tasks in reading disabled children. *Learning Disabilities Quarterly,* *2*(3):17-23, 1979.

Trimble, M.R. *Post-Traumatic Neurosis: From Railway Spine to the Whiplash.* New York, John Wiley and Sons, 1981.

Vallier, F.J., and Wertz, R.T. Recognition memory in brain injured adults. Paper presented American-Speech-Hearing Association, San Francisco, November, 1978.

van Woerkon, T.C.A.M., Minderhound, J.M., and Nicolai, G.G. Neurotransmitters in the treatment of patients with severe head injuries. *European Neurology, 21:*227-241, 1982.

Vygotsky, L.S. In M. Cole, J. Steiner, S. Scribner, and E. Souberman (Eds.), *Mind in society: The development of higher psychological processes.* Cambridge, Harvard University Press, 1978.

Wada, J.A., and Rasmussen, T. Intracarotid injection of sodium amytal for the lateralization of cerebral speech dominance: Experimental and clinical observations. *Journal of Neurosurgery,* *17:*266-282, 1960.

Warren, L.R., Hubbard, D.J., and Knox, A.W. Short-term memory scan in normal individuals and individuals with aphasia. *Journal of Speech and Hearing Research, 20:*497-509, 1977.

Waterhouse, L., and Fein, D. Language skills in developmentally disabled children. *Brain and Language, 15:*307-333, 1982.

Wetzel, C.D., and Squire, L.R. Cued recall in anterograde amnesia. *Brain and Language, 15:*70-81, 1982.

Whitaker, H.A., and Ojemann, G.A. Lateralization of higher cortical functions: A critique. *Annals of the New York Academy of Sciences, 299:*459-473, 1977.

Wilson, P.B. Software selection and use in language and cognitive retraining. *Cognitive Rehabilitation 1*(1):9-10, 1983.

Yakolev, P. Motility, behavior and the brain. *Journal of Nervous and Mental Disease, 107:*313, 1948.

Yorkston, K. Treatment of right hemisphere damaged patients: A panel discussion. Clinical Aphasiology Conference Proceedings, Kerrville, TX, pp. 281-283. Minneapolis, BRK Publishers, 1981.

Zaidel, E. A technique for presenting lateralized visual input with prolonged exposure. *Vision Research, 15:*283-289, 1975.

Zaidel, E., and Sperry, R.W. Some long-term motor effects of cerebral commissurotomy in man. *Neuropsychologia, 15:*193-204, 1977.

Author Index

Subject Index

Page numbers in *italics* refer to illustrations; (t) indicates a table.

DATE DUE

DEMCO NO. 38-298